BOB BOOKS®

Sight Words

WORKBOOK

Scholastic Inc.

Dear Parent,

Help your child build their reading skills with sight words! **Sight words**, also known as **high-frequency words**, are words children encounter again and again in their reading materials. Some can be sounded out, but many cannot. Being able to recognize these words "on sight" increases your child's confidence and fluency when reading.

Bob Books: Sight Words Workbook makes learning these sight words fun! Kids have many opportunities to practice their high-frequency words through tracing, writing, word mazes, matching activities, and of course, reading stories!

This workbook is perfect for children who are learning to read and can sound out CVC (consonant-vowel-consonant) words. It can be used alongside the Bob Books Stage 2 box sets, or on its own.

The sight words are presented in a specific order, so children learn the most frequently used words first. Because the activities are cumulative, you and your child should **move through the activities in order**. For each activity, read the instructions to your child. Then help them get started and be available to answer questions. Once your child has completed the workbook, make sure to hang up the **achievement certificate** so they can be proud of their hard work!

We hope you have fun learning sight words with Mat, Sam, Dot, Mac, and all the other Bob Books friends!

— The Bob Books team

ISBN 979-8-225-00475-0   10 9 8 7 6 5 4 3 2 1   25 26 27 28 29
Printed in the U.S.A. 40   First printing 2025
Read aloud icon © Getty Images   Cover art by Amy Jindra and Karen Wall
Cover design by Dynamo   Book design by Dynamo

Table of Contents

Welcome to the World of Bob Books!

Color the Bob Books friends below.
Then draw a picture of yourself!

the

Trace the word.

the

Write it two times.

A dog is in **the** tub.

Sam thinks his new pen is **the** best! Color all the papers that have *the*.

and

Trace the word.

and

Write it two times.

Fill in the boxes to spell **and**. Read the phrases.

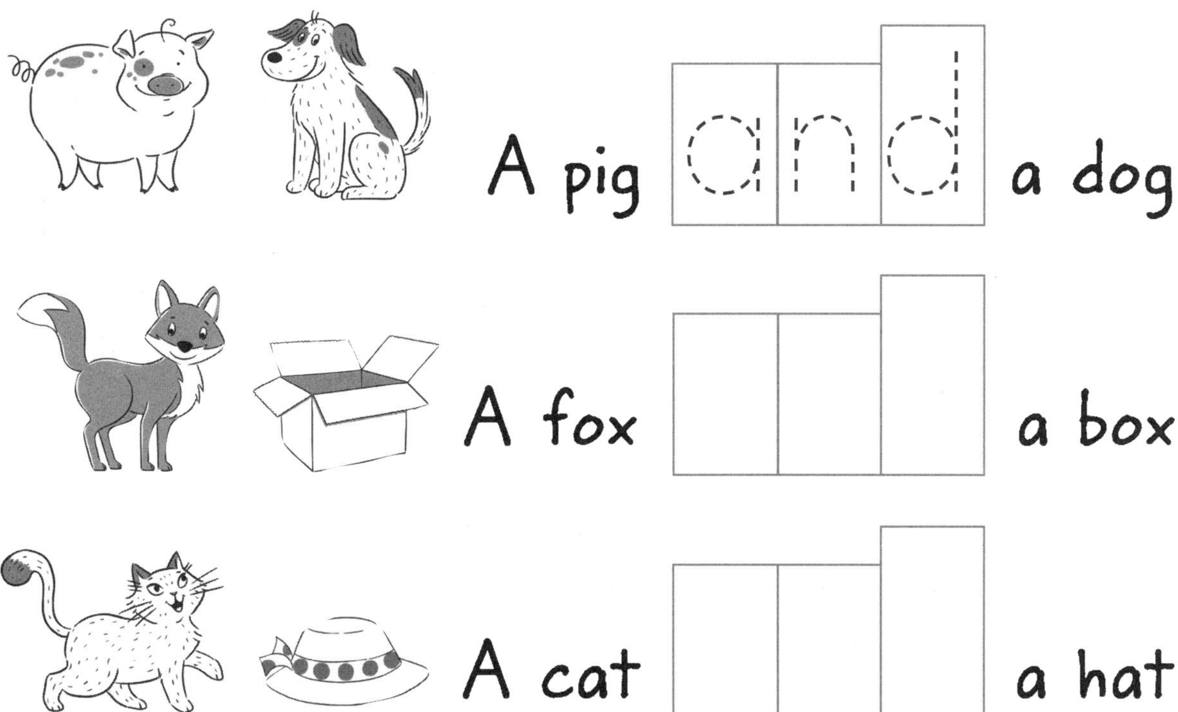

A pig **and** a dog

A fox a box

A cat a hat

Circle and Underline

Read the sentences. Circle *the*. Underline *and*.

A pig and a dog dig.

The pig runs.   The dog runs.

The pig and the dog jump in.

to

Trace the word.

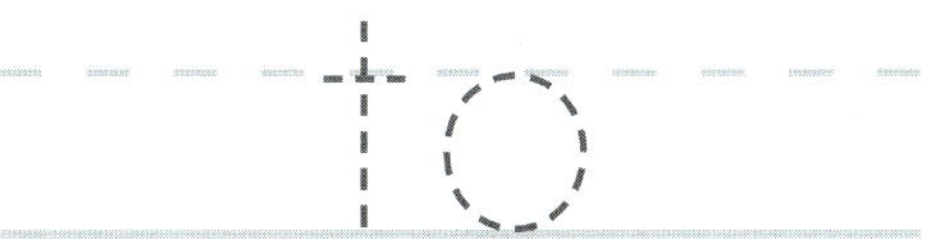

Write it three times.

Read each word. Circle **to**. Cross out other words.

to   the

and   to

to   the

to   and

go

Trace the word.

Write it three times.

The cat wants to **go** in the car with the rat! Start at the cat. Draw lines to the word *go* until the cat reaches the car.

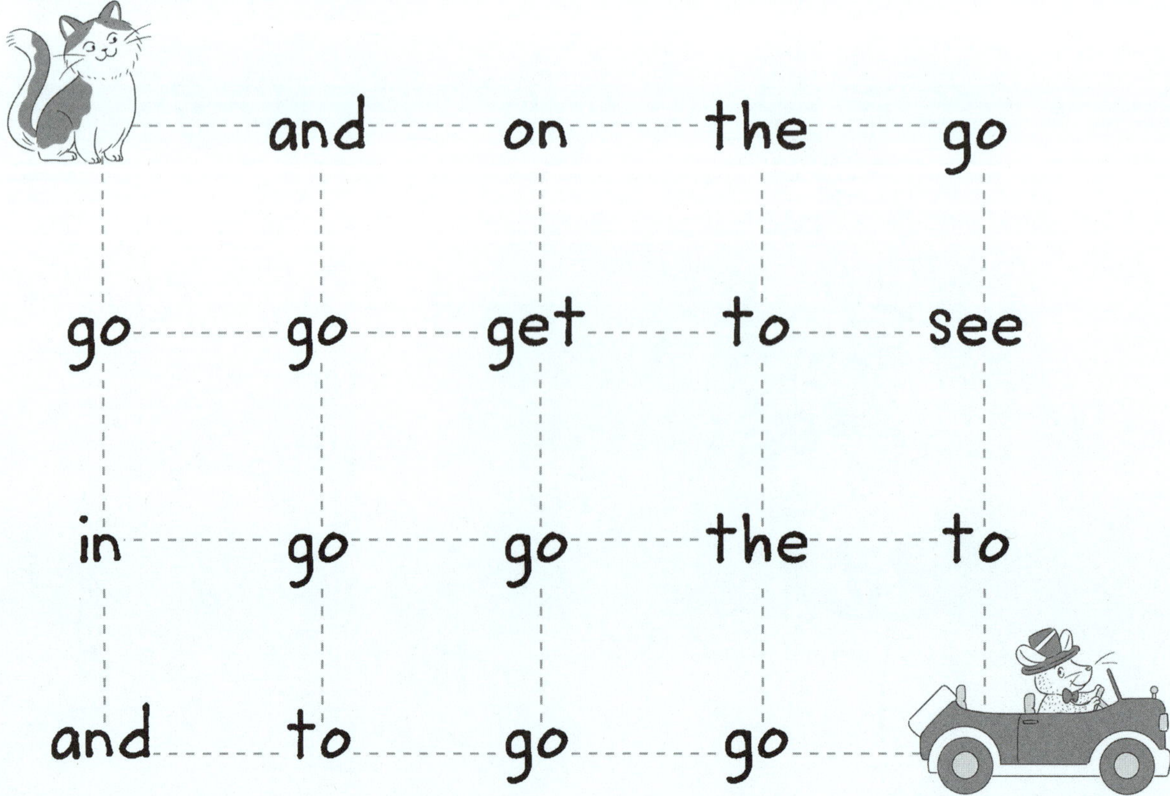

see

Trace the word.

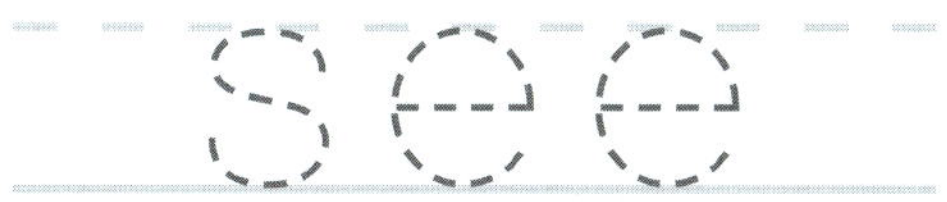

Write it two times.

Kim can **see** a pile of balls. Color all the balls with *see* on them.

in

Trace the word.

in

Write it three times.

Start at *i*. Trace the line to connect *i* to *n*. Say "iiiiiiin" as you do it.

i — — — — — — — — — — n

i — — — — — — n

i — — — n

in

Color by Sight Word

Mat sees a hot-air balloon! Use the color code to color the picture.

to — red

go — blue

see — green

in — yellow

Story Time!

Color the pictures.

Review the sight words.

Read the story.

the   and   to

go   see   in

Red and Ned

Ned and Red go in the bus.

Go, bus, go!

Red and Ned get off.

Red can see Dad.

Ned runs to Mom.

Red and Ned go.

you

Trace the word.

y o u

Write it two times.

What makes you, you? Decorate the word **you** so it feels like **you**!

YOU

my

Trace the word.

my

Write it two times.

Jin says, "I love **my** teddy bear!" Color the teddy bears that have the word *my*.

to

my

go

my

see

my

for

Trace the word.

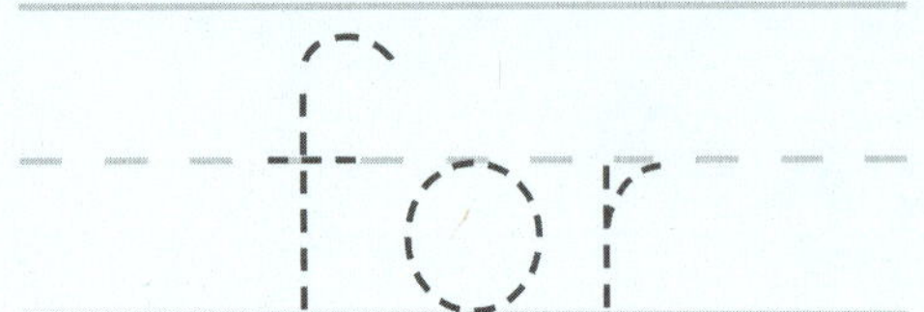

Write it two times.

Mac has invitations **for** his friends. Fill in the boxes to spell *for*.

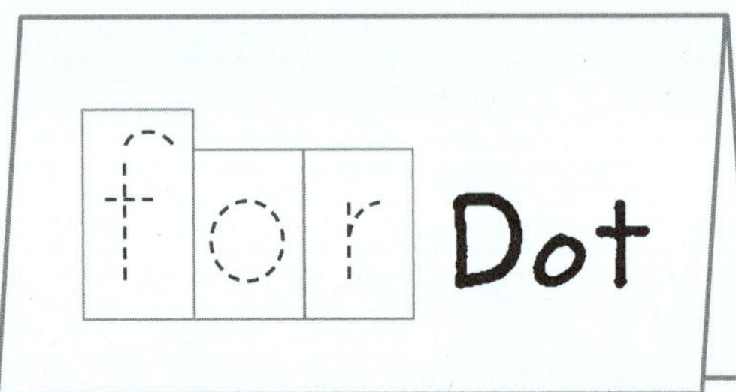

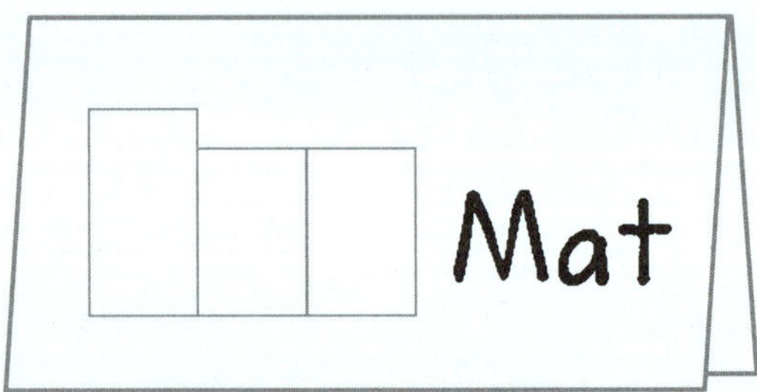

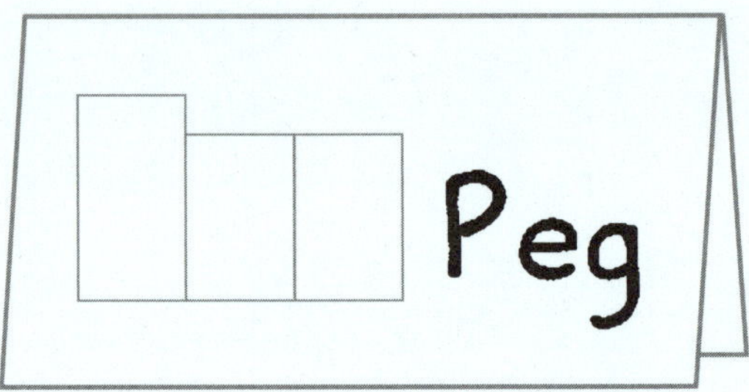

get

Trace the word.

Write it two times.

Mag took Dot's hat! Help Dot **get** her hat. Follow ***get*** through the maze.

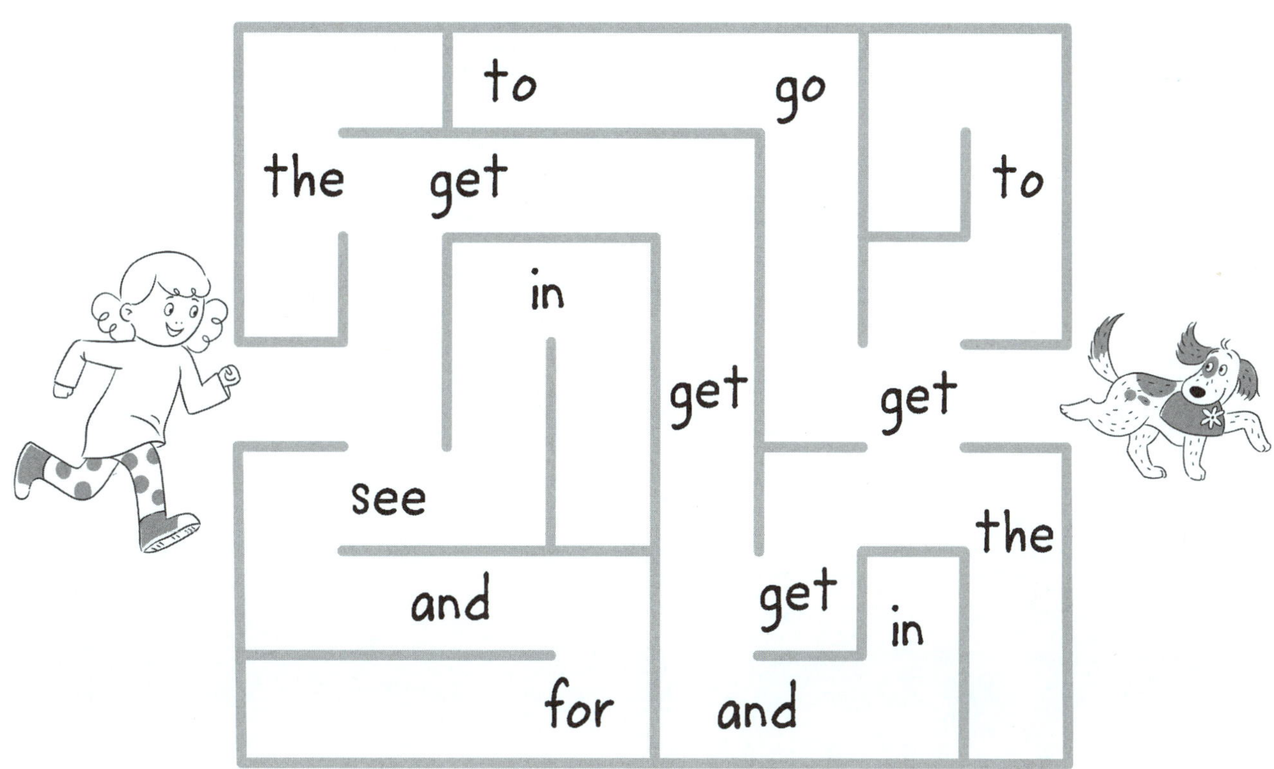

Silly Writing

Jaz loves being creative! Help her write these words in silly ways.

Write **you** really BIG.

Write **my** very small.

Write **for** in a fancy way.

Write **get** however you like!

as

Trace the word.

as

Write it three times.

Read the sentences. Circle the word **as**.

The hat is as big as the box.

The hen is as soft as the cat.

of

Trace the word.

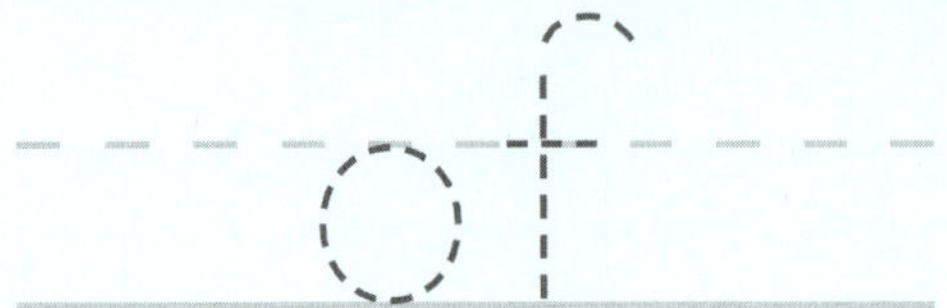

Write it three times.

Dot has a lot **of** hats! Draw a line from Dot to each hat that has *of*.

on

Trace the word.

on

Write it three times.

Color in the word **on**. Draw a line to the picture where Mag is **on** a mat.

on

off

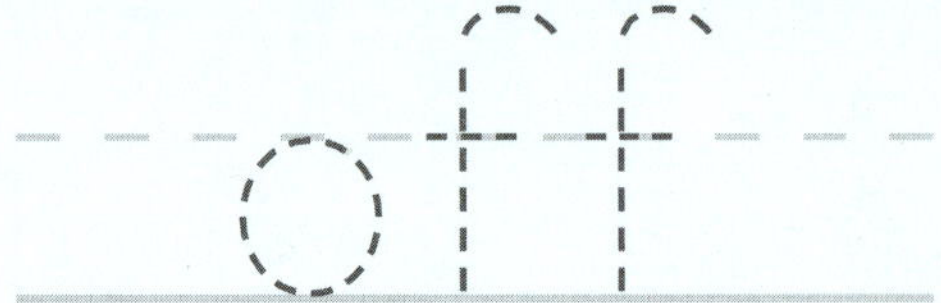

Trace the word.

Write it two times.

Sam needs to turn **off** the light. Start at Sam. Draw lines to the word **off** until Sam gets to the light.

Words and Shapes

Jin is drawing with sidewalk chalk. Draw these shapes around her words.

Story Time!

you	my	for	get
as	of	on	off

Rex Sits

Tex has a hat, a cat, and a dog.

Max is not as big as Rex.

Rex sits on Max!

"You can not sit on my cat, Rex! Get off!"

Rex has a lot of licks for Tex!

Trace the word.

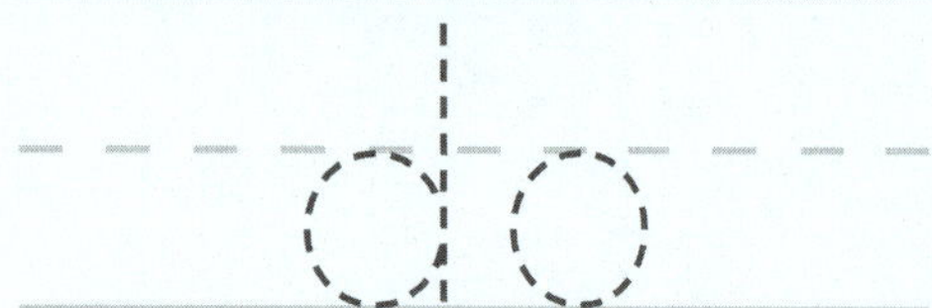

Write it three times.

Help Sam **do** his chores! Draw x's through the tiles with the word **do**. Can you find four in a row?

do	you	do	to	off
my	do	do	as	do
do	go	do	you	to
to	on	do	in	do

at

Trace the word.

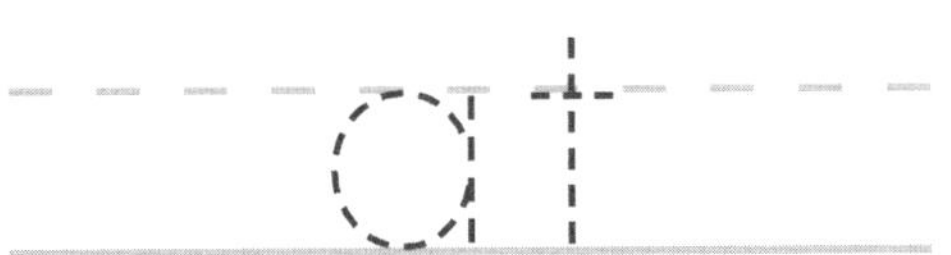

Write it three times.

Read the words. Circle **at**. Cross out other words.

be

Trace the word.

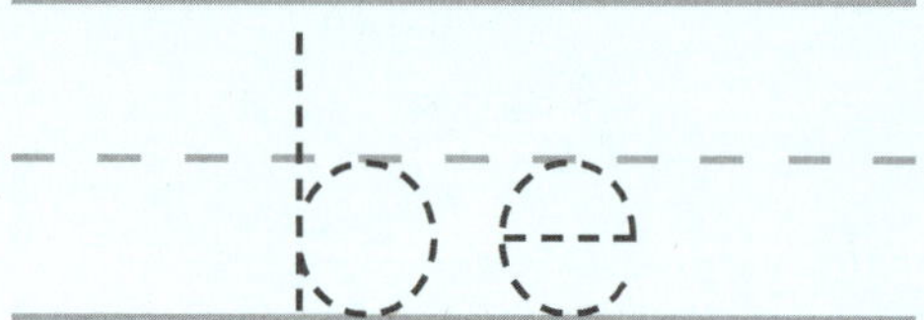

Write it two times.

There seem to **be** lots of fish in the pond today! Circle all the fish that have the word **be**.

all

Trace the word.

Write it two times.

Use **all** the colors you have to decorate the word *all*!

Word Match

Mat was trying to do a card trick, but he dropped all the cards! Each card has a match. Read the words. Color each card and its match the same color.

we

Trace the word.

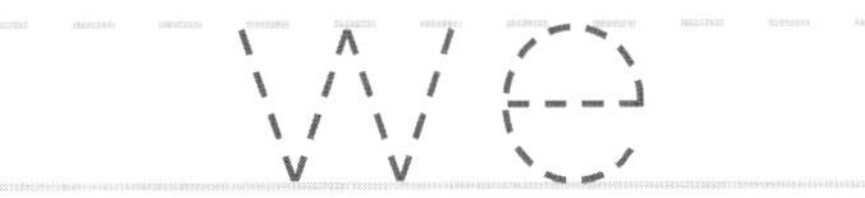

Write it three times.

We pet the dog.

Read the sentences. Circle the word **we**.

We can sit.

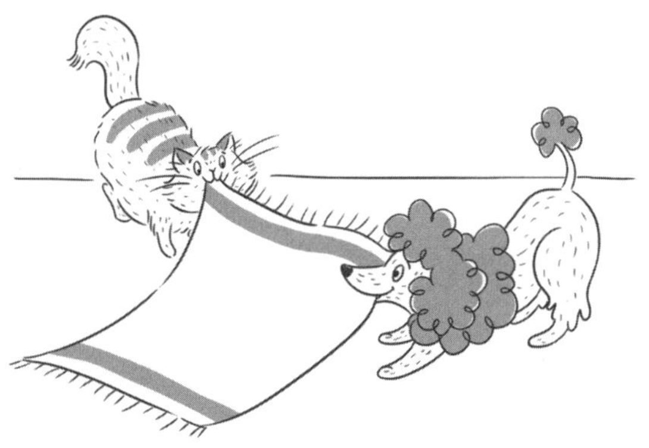

We tug and tug.

was

Trace the word.

was

Write it two times.

The cat **was** wet.

Mac **was** splashing at the beach. He saw a crab but it ran off! Start at Mac. Draw lines to the word **was** until Mac finds the crab.

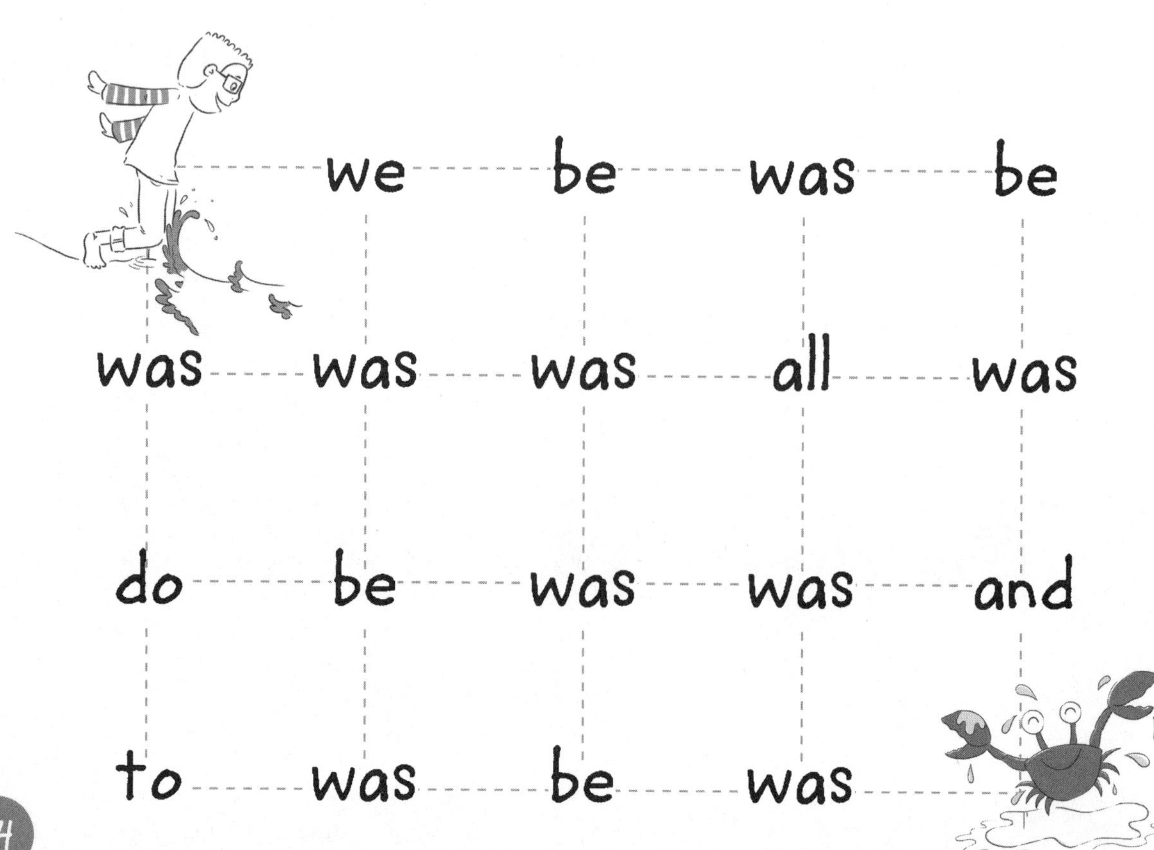

so

Trace the word.

so

Write it three times.

Read the words. Circle **so**. Cross out other words.

so

do

so

so

we

we

so

at

or

Trace the word.

Write it three times.

Is it a cat **or** a dog?

Fill in the boxes to spell the word *or*. Read the sentences.

Sam can hop ☐☐ jump.

Did Bud sit ☐☐ run?

Silly Writing

Help Nic paint a mural with some silly writing!

Write **we** really BIG.

Write **was** very small.

Write **so** using dots.

Write **or** in **bubble** letters.

Color the pictures.

Review the sight words.

Read the story.

> do   at   be   all
>
> we   was   so   or

We Can Do It!

Dot was at a hill.

Go fast so you can get to the top, Dot!

Dot fell.

Will Dot go or stop?

Dot can do it.

Mat will be a pal!

We can all do it!

but

Trace the word.

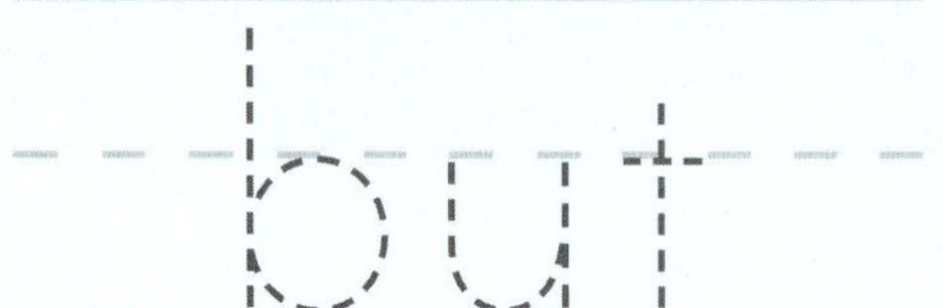

but

Write it two times.

Pig is in the mud,
but Hen is not.

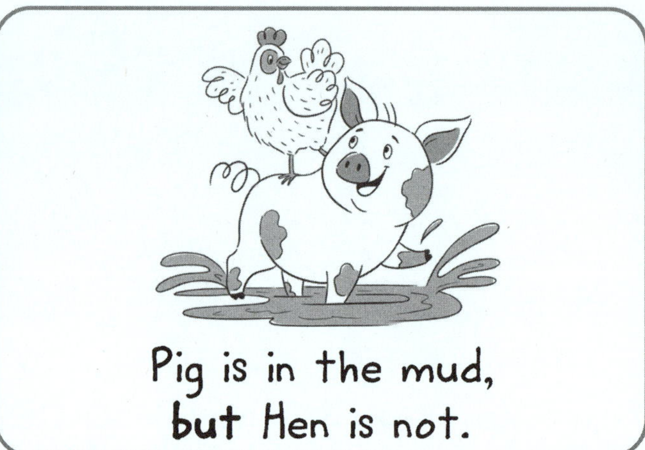

Ted wants to fix his toy, **but** he needs more tools. Follow the word ***but*** through the maze until Ted gets to his tools.

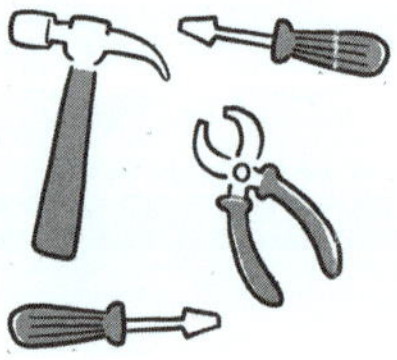

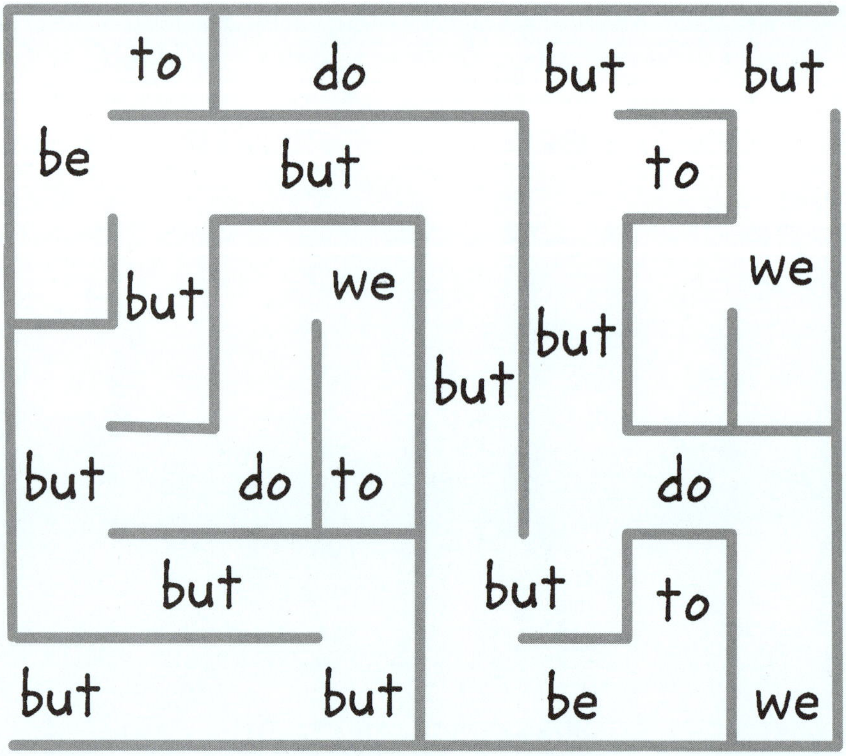

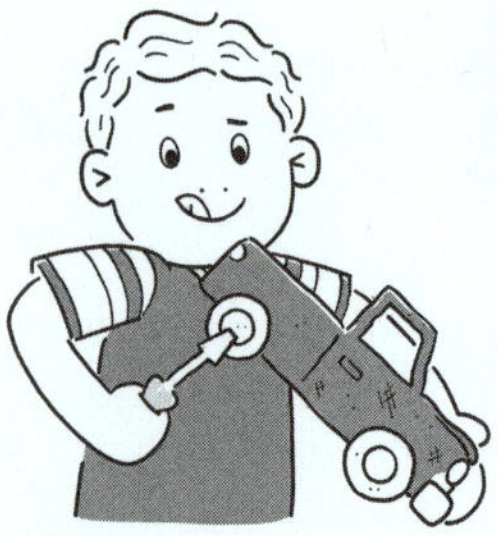

with

Trace the word.

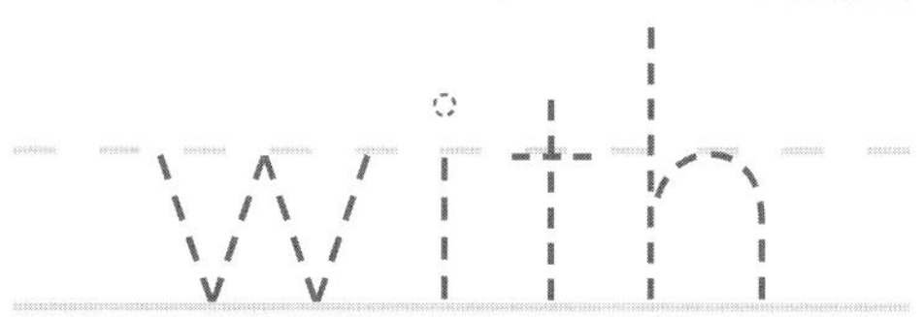

Write it two times.

Mit loves to play **with** butterflies. Draw a line from Mit to each butterfly that has the word **with**.

Trace the word.

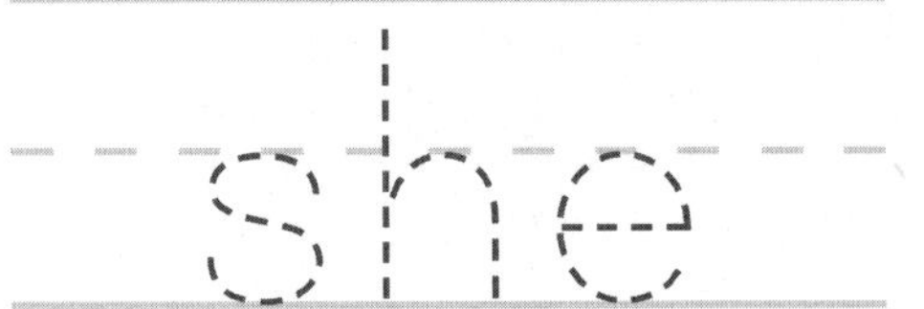

Write it two times.

Read the sentences. Circle the word *she*.

She has a red hat.

She pats the cat.

he

Trace the word.

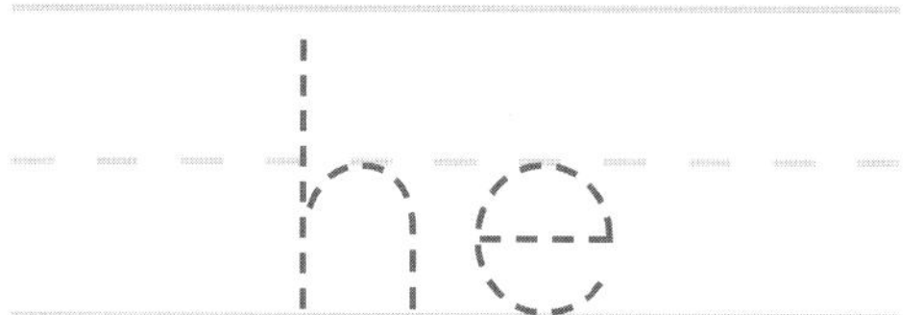

Write it three times.

Ben needs to feed his hen. Start at Ben. Draw lines to the word **he** until Ben reaches his hen.

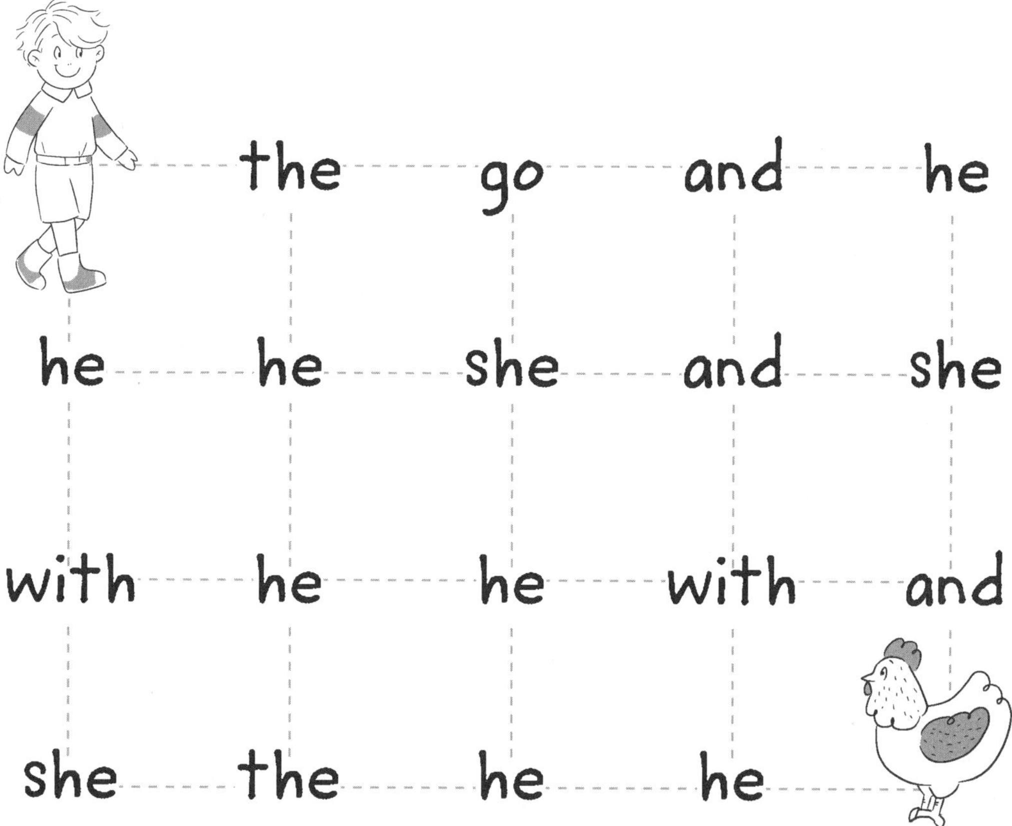

Word Search

Find each word and circle it.
Each word is hidden two times.

but   with   she   he

c q b u t v r s h e
d w j k w b c k y z
g h e f w o n d m f
j w i t h v n b k y
a f d s r k x n m s
h e d n j
k l b u t
z w i t h
s h e j d

are

Trace the word.

are

The bugs **are** in the box.

Write it two times.

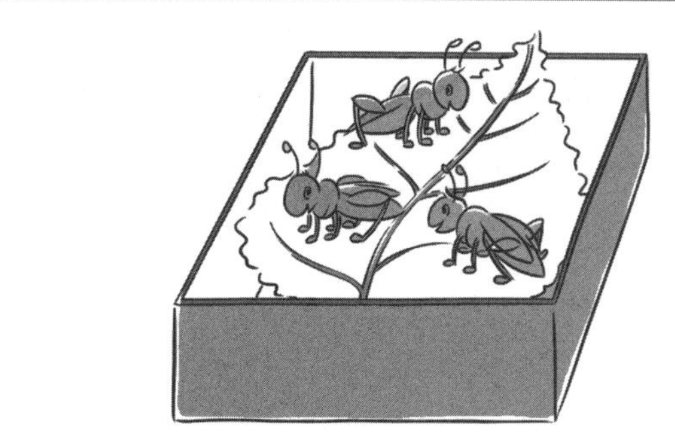

There **are** lots of bugs where Mat, Sam, and Dot **are** playing! Draw a line from each bug to the word ***are***.

are

are

at

as

are

to

and

all

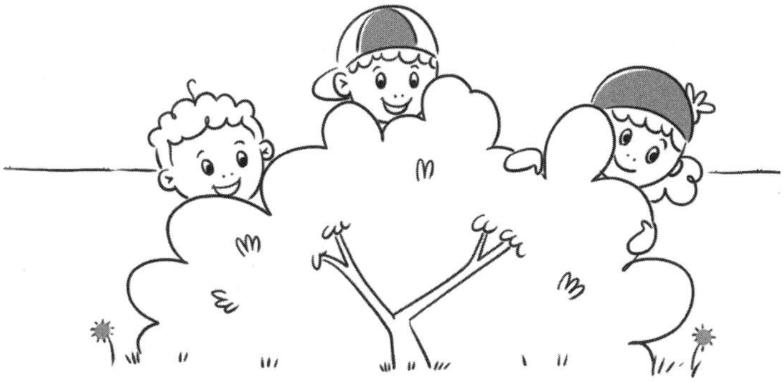

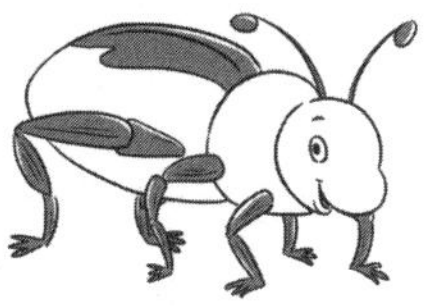

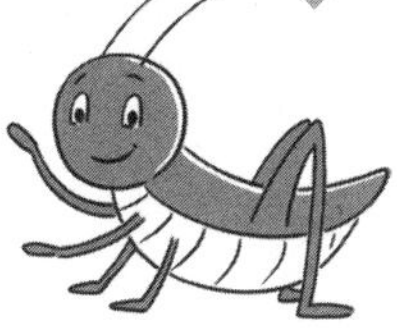

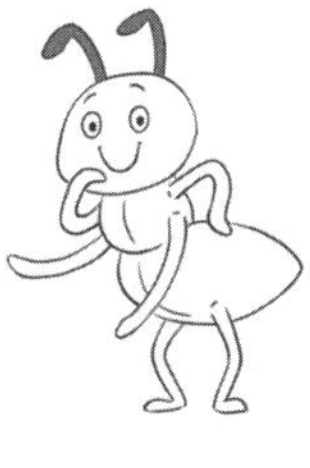

had

Trace the word.

had

Write it two times.

Fill in the boxes to spell *had*. Read the sentences.

Nic ☐☐☐ a pot.

Ben ☐☐☐ a jug.

now

Trace the word.

n o w

Write it two times.

Now the sun is up.

Read each word. Circle **now**. Cross out other words.

out

Trace the word.

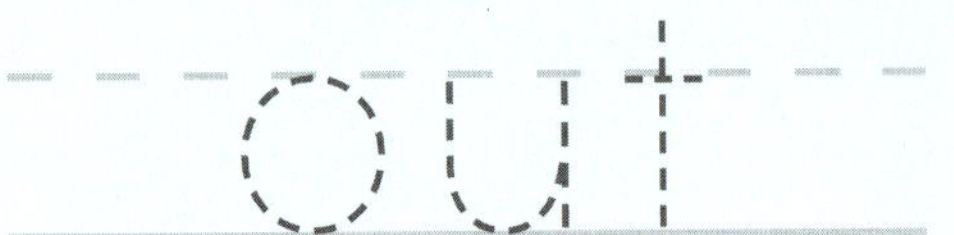

Write it two times.

Color in the word **out**. Draw a line to the picture where Ted and Peg are **out** of the water.

Word Match

Jig is playing a game with his ducks. Each duck has a match. Read the words. Color each duck and its match the same color.

Story Time!

Color the pictures.

Review the sight words.

Read the story.

> but with she he
>
> are had now out

In the Mud

Ann's cat got in the mud.
He is a mess!

Now six cats are in the mud!

But Ann had a plan.

She got the cats out.

She helps with the mud. Rub-a-dub!

them

Trace the word.

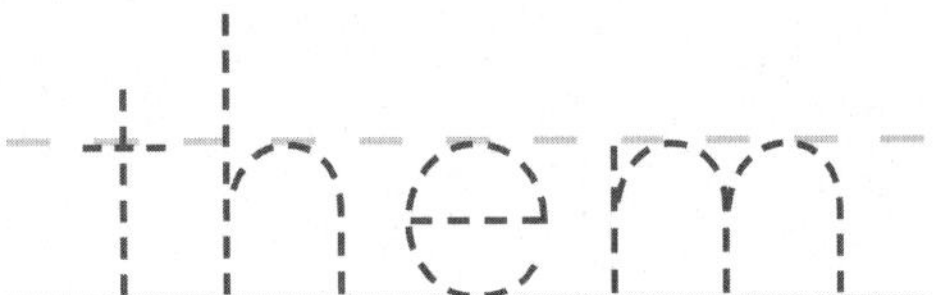

Write it two times.

Bet loves her pets! Help her get to **them**. Follow the word *them* through the maze to get to the pets.

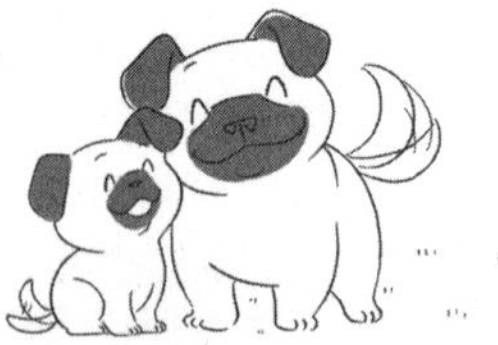

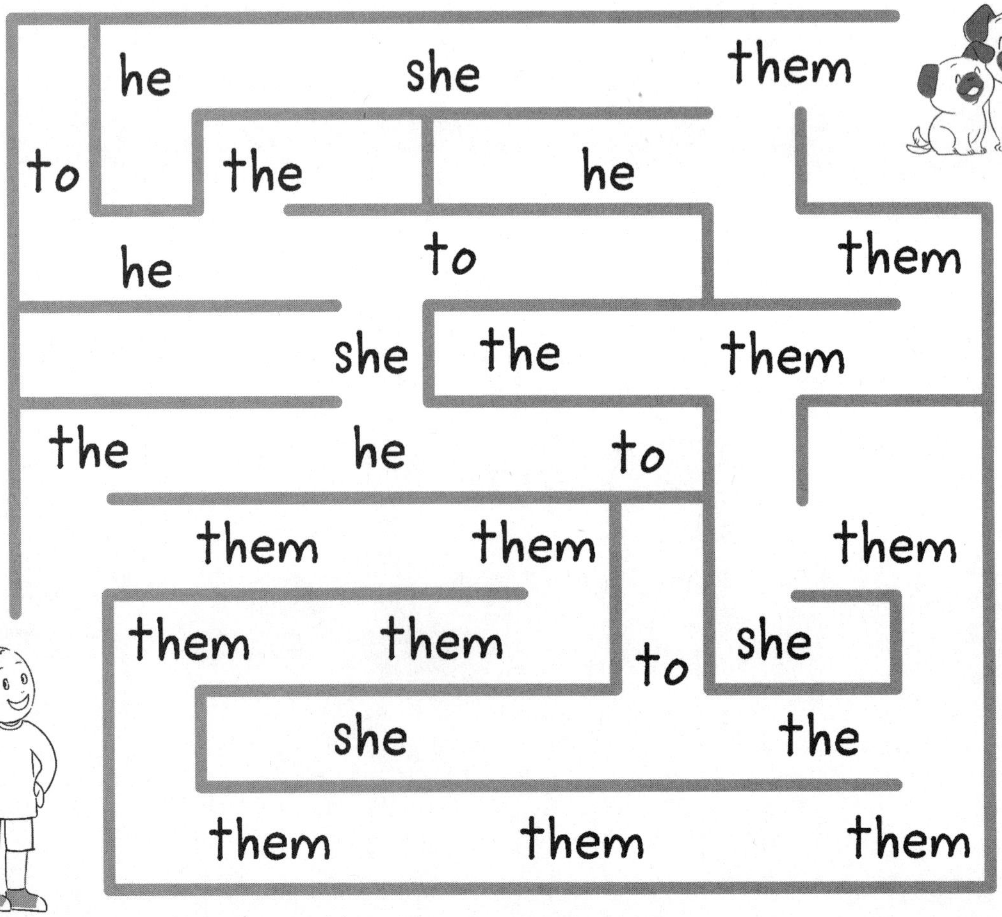

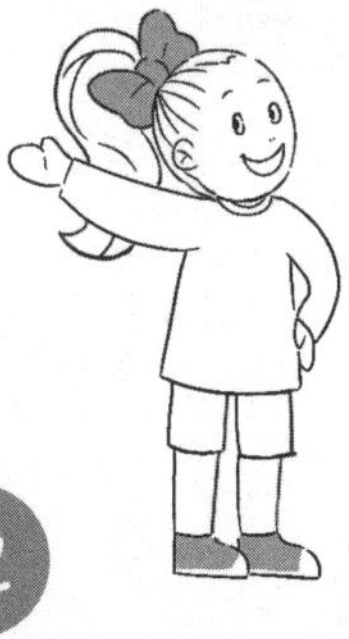

there

Trace the word.

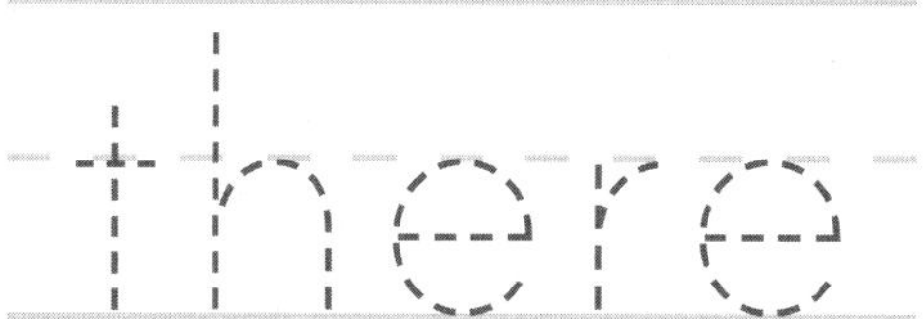

Write it two times.

Read the sentences. Circle *there*.

There is 1 bag.

There are 2 hats.

they

Trace the word.

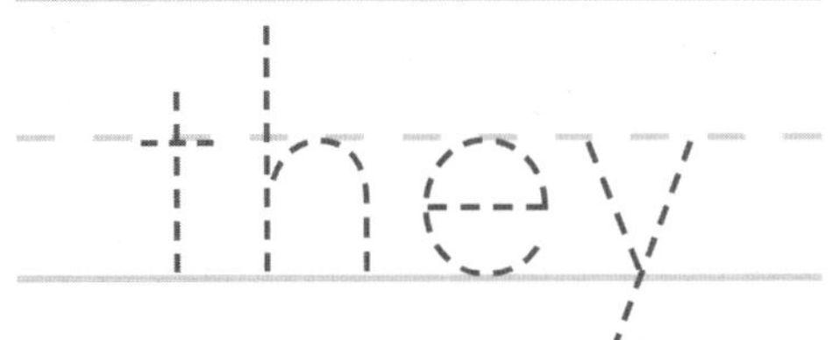

Write it two times.

They love to dance! Find the word **_they_** hidden two times on the dance floor. Color in the squares.

d	q	e	s	j	a
o	f	t	e	y	n
f	l	h	a	t	k
c	m	e	l	h	i
n	v	y	e	e	t
z	u	f	e	y	b

this

Trace the word.

this

Write it two times.

Fill in the blanks to spell **this**. Read the sentences.

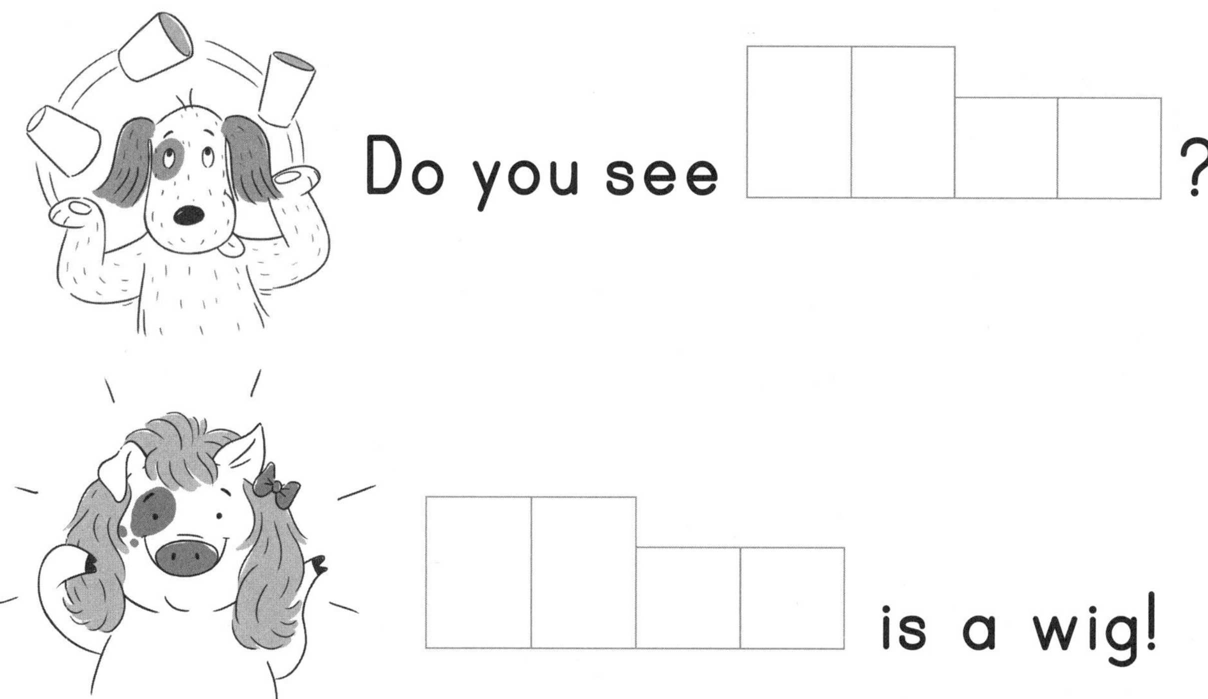

Words in Shapes

It's Mat's birthday! Help Dot and Sam sort the gifts. The four gift bags at the top each have a match below. Find the matching gifts and circle the matching sight words.

have

Trace the word.

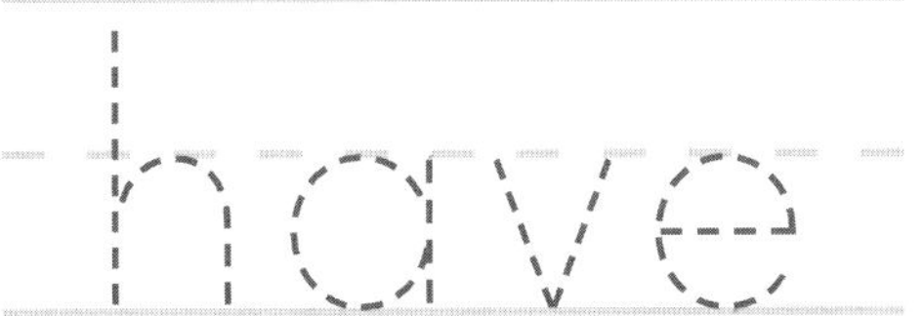

Write it two times.

Jig has to **have** a bath! Start at Jig. Draw lines to the word **have** until Jig can hop in the tub.

look

Trace the word.

Write it two times.

Nic and Jaz **look** at the nest.

Look has two o's in the middle that **look** like a pair of eyes. Color in the word **look**, then decorate the glasses!

saw

Trace the word.

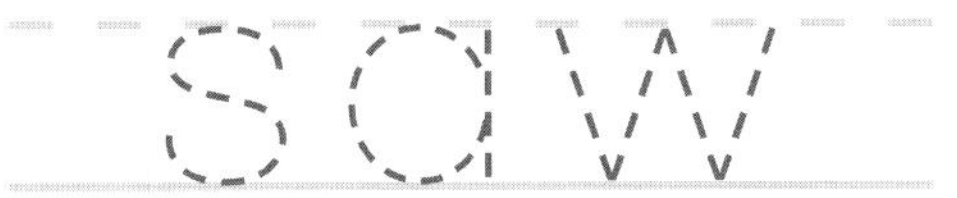

Write it two times.

Read each word. Circle **saw**. Cross out other words.

up

Trace the word.

up

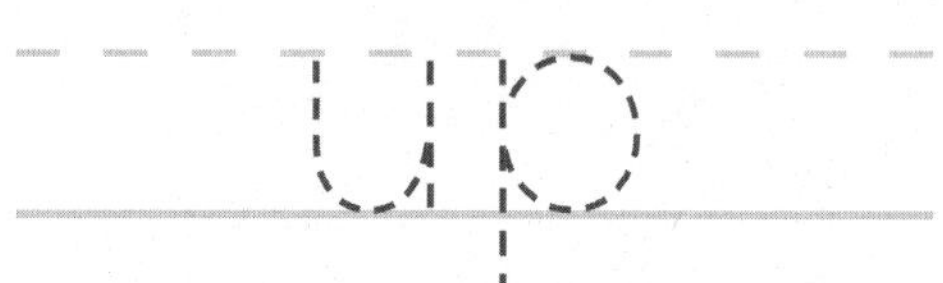

Write it three times.

Dot went up.

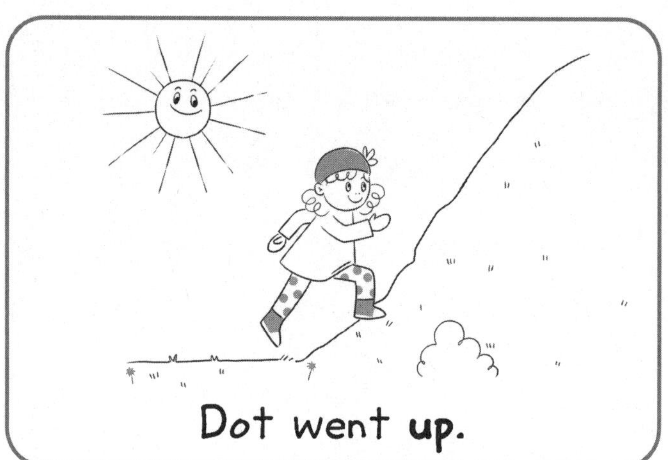

Kim's and Jin's kites are flying **up** in the sky! Trace the lines **up** to the kites, then write one letter in each kite to spell the word ***up***.

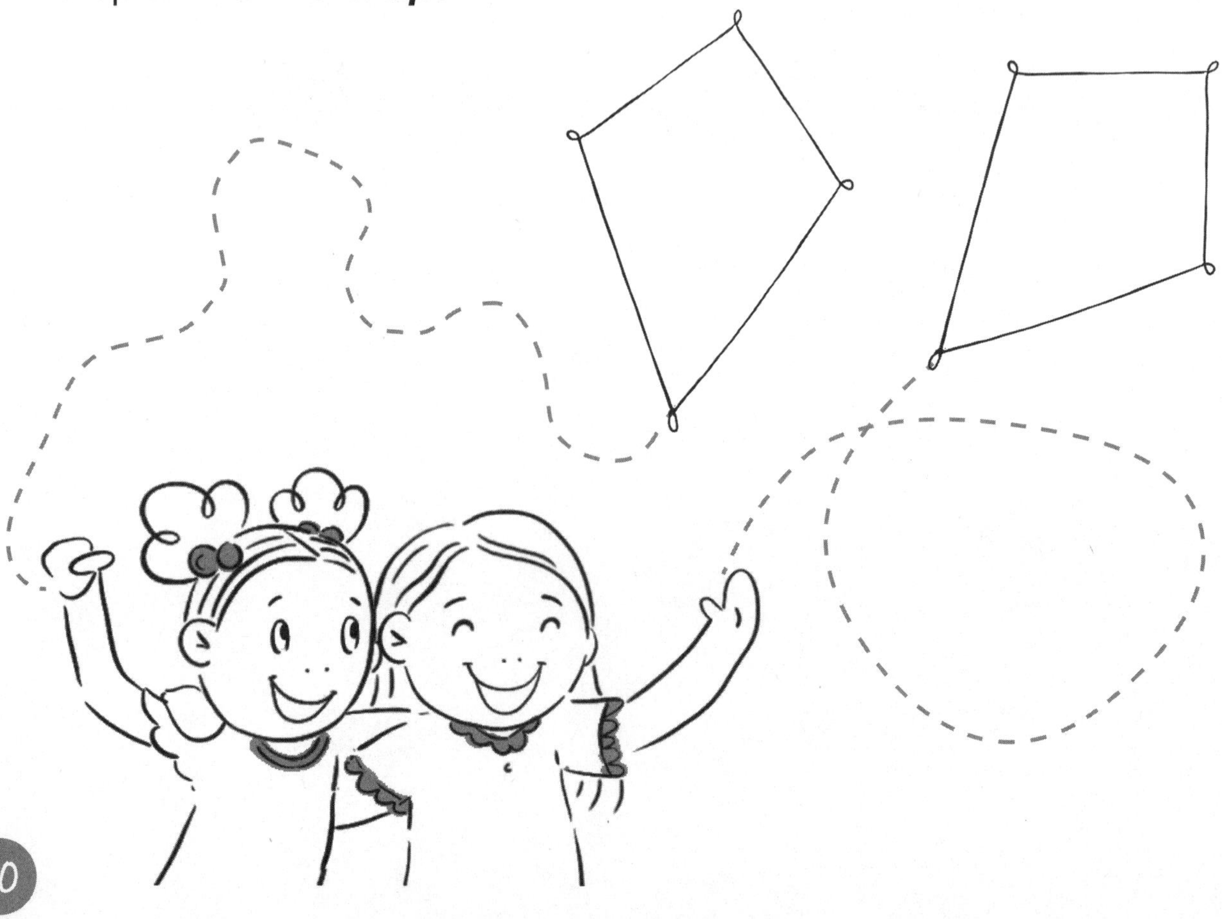

Word Pairs

Ted is painting model cars and trucks. Each word is on two vehicles. Color the vehicles with matching words the same color.

Story Time!

Color the pictures.

Review the sight words.

Read the story.

them	there	they	this
have	look	saw	up

Dot's Pals

This is Dot's hen. Dot saw eggs.

Pals pop out! There are six of them.

Look! They tug a lot.

They hop up on Dot.

They have tons of fun!

were

Trace the word.

were

Peg and Ted **were** on the bus.

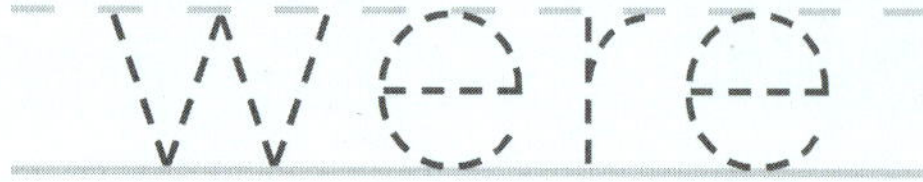

Write it two times.

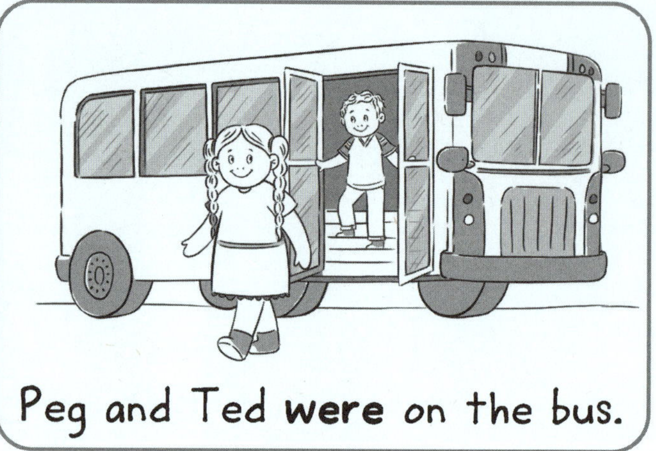

Help the bus get the kids home. Follow the word ***were*** through the maze.

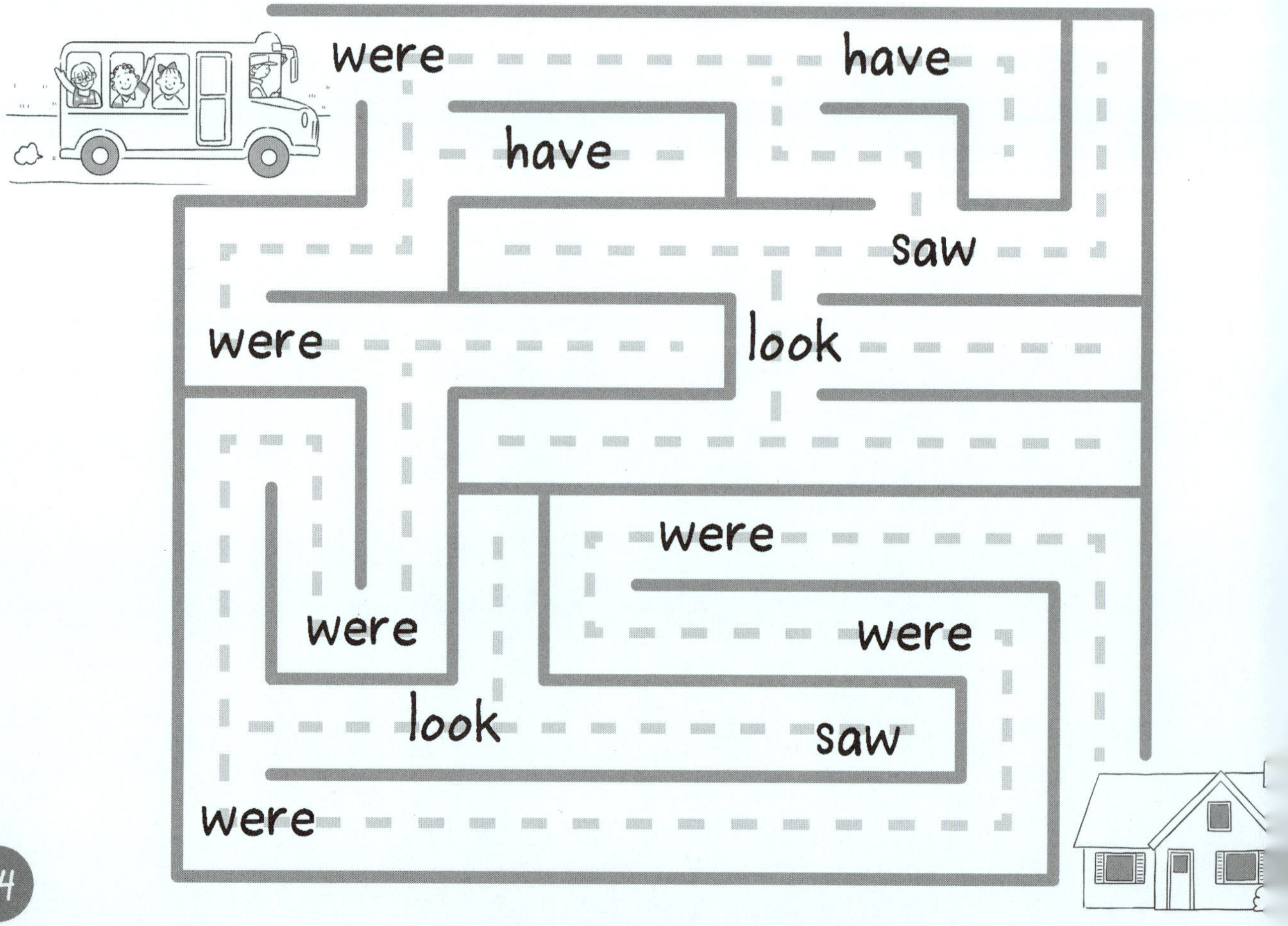

what

Trace the word.

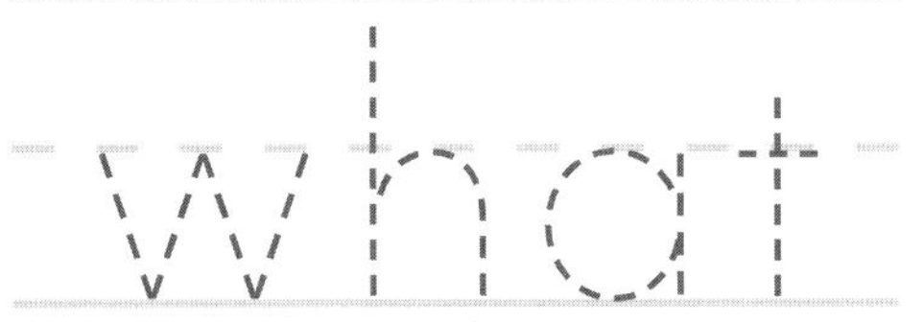

Write it two times.

Fill in the blanks to spell **what**. Read the sentences.

Look ☐☐☐☐ the dog can do!

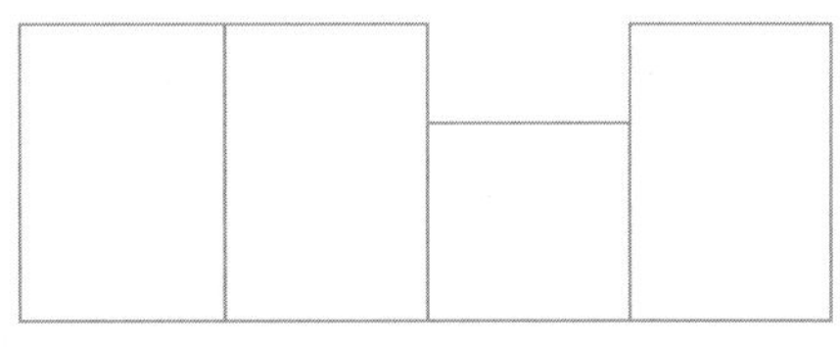

☐☐☐☐ is out there?

when

Trace the word.

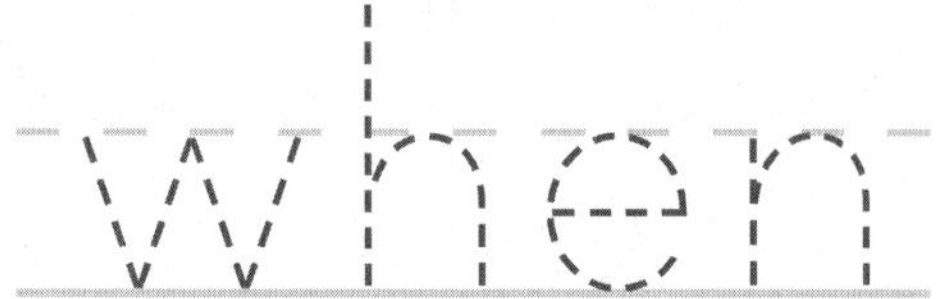

Write it two times.

When it's dinnertime, Ben feeds his cat. Start at Ben.
Draw lines to the word **when** until Ben reaches his cat.

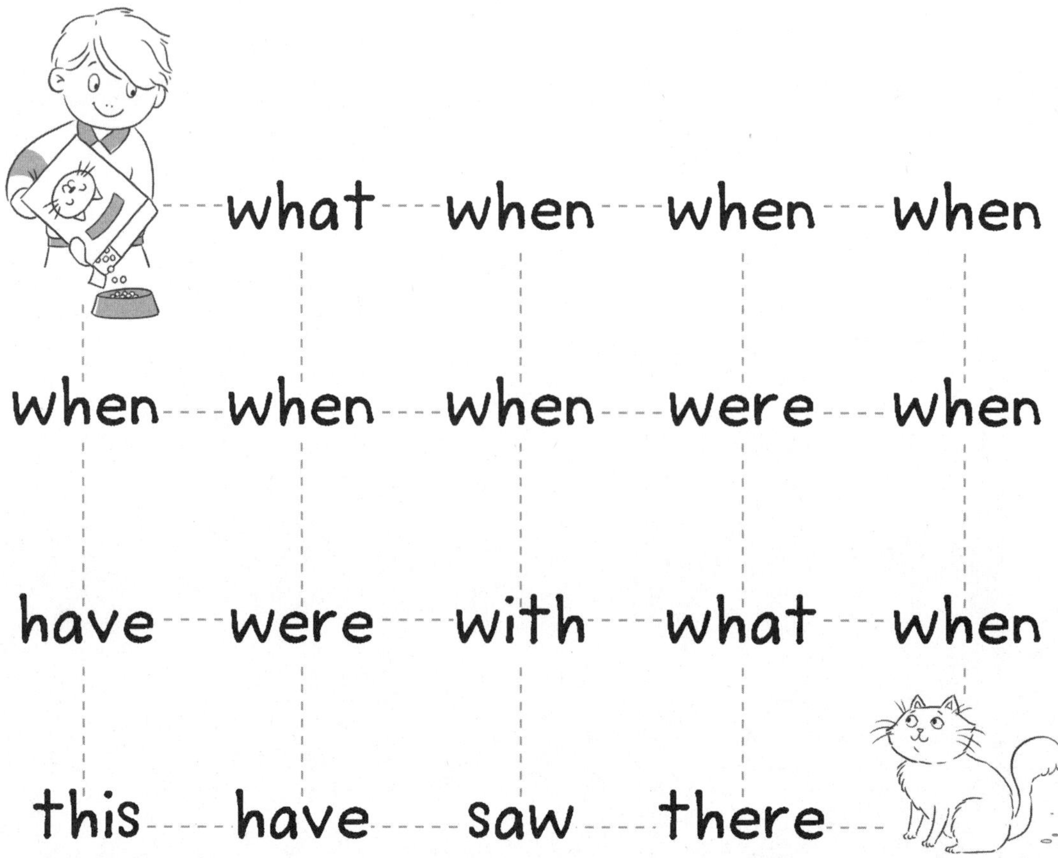

who

Trace the word.

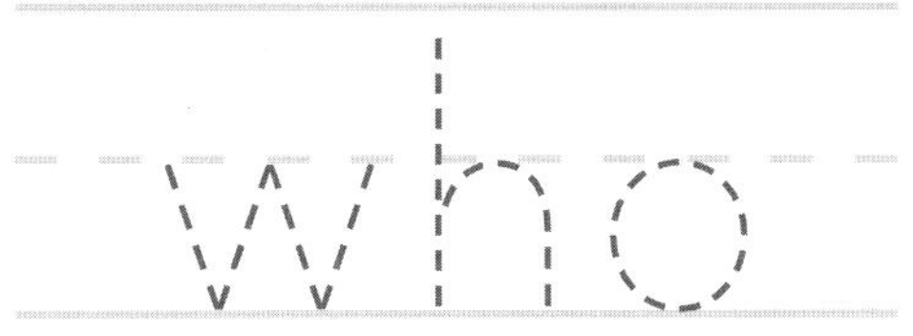

Write it two times.

Color in the word *who*. Draw a line to the person **who** has a flag.

Word Search

Find each word and circle it.
Each word is hidden two times.

were   what   when   who

b a w h o g i l r y
w h a t h a w e r e
c o r w h a t m n d
w h e n d r s t a l
f i v p w e r e o d
t a y r n
w h o f p
z i m d r
j w h e n

how

Trace the word.

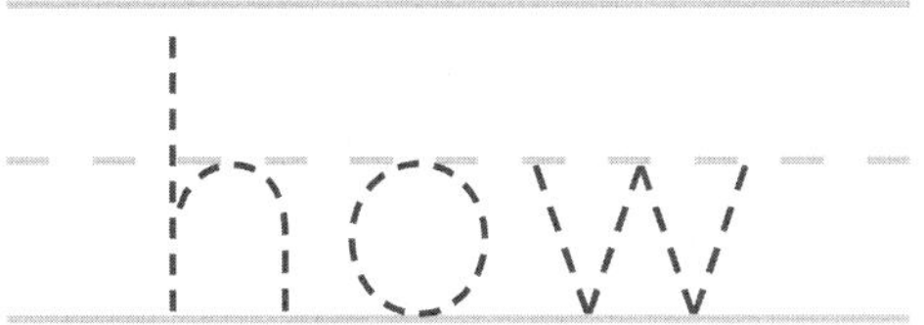

Write it two times.

Use your imagination and decorate the word **how** however you like!

his

Trace the word.

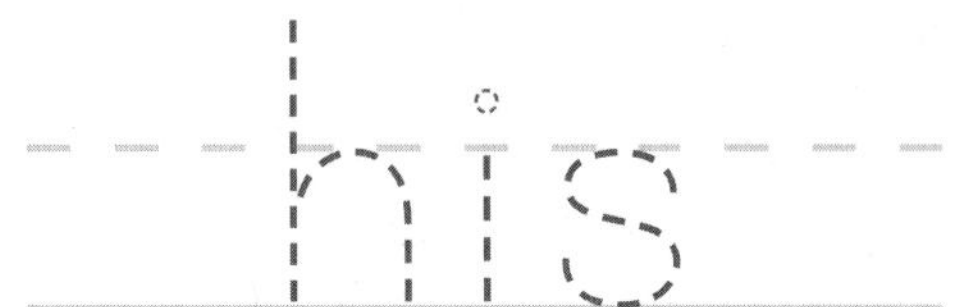

Write it two times.

Read each word. Circle **his**. Cross out other words.

have

his

was

look

how

his

his

was

out

then

Trace the word.

Write it two times.

Read the sentences. Circle the word *then*.

Hen hops in bed.

Then she naps.

The jug tips.

Then Mit gets milk.

that

Trace the word.

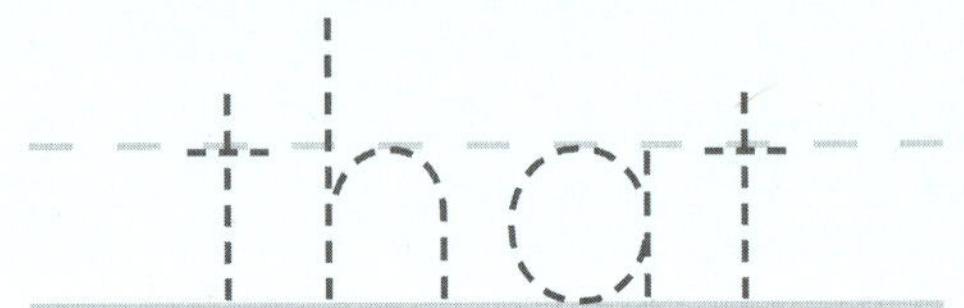

Write it two times.

Catch **that** rat! Draw lines to the word *that* until the cat gets to the rat.

Silly Writing

Sam is always doing flips. He likes flipping his writing, too! Can you write like Sam?

Write **or** and **we** backward.

Write **so** sideways.

Write **was** upside down!

Color the pictures.

Review the sight words.

Read the story.

were	what	when	who
how	his	then	that

A Big Hop

Ted and Peg were on a trip.

What was that? Who was that? A frog!

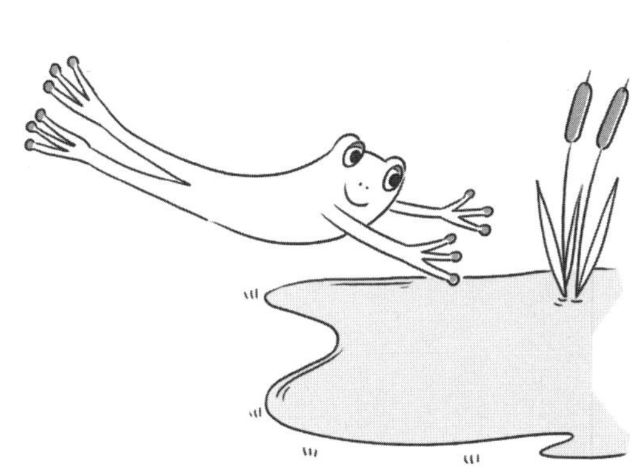

It did a BIG hop
when it saw them.

How did the frog do that?
With its BIG legs!

Then they swam with the frog. Fun!

Trace the word.

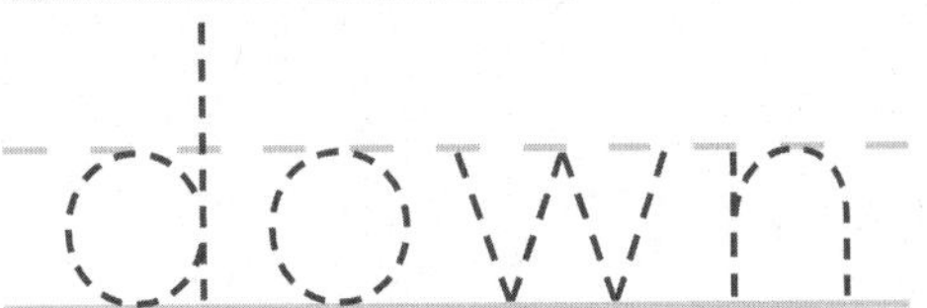

Write it two times.

Ted's ball rolled **down** the stairs! Write one letter on each stair to spell **down**.

from

Trace the word.

from

It is **from** Mac.

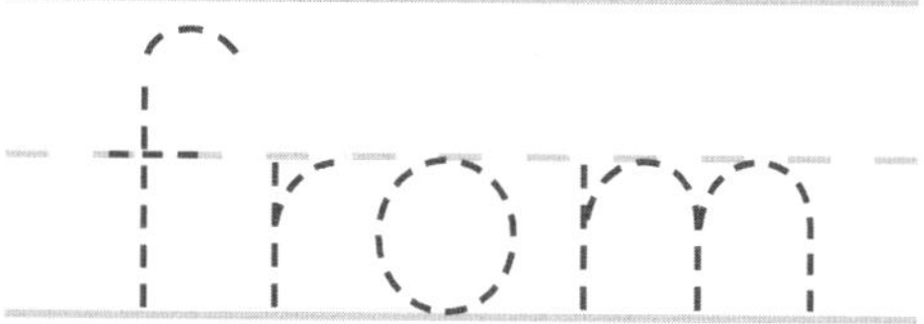

Write it two times.

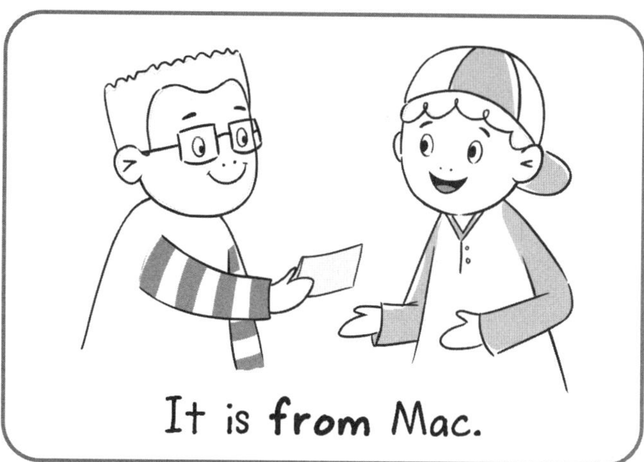

Help Sam go **from** one side to the other. Color the rocks with ***from*** on them.

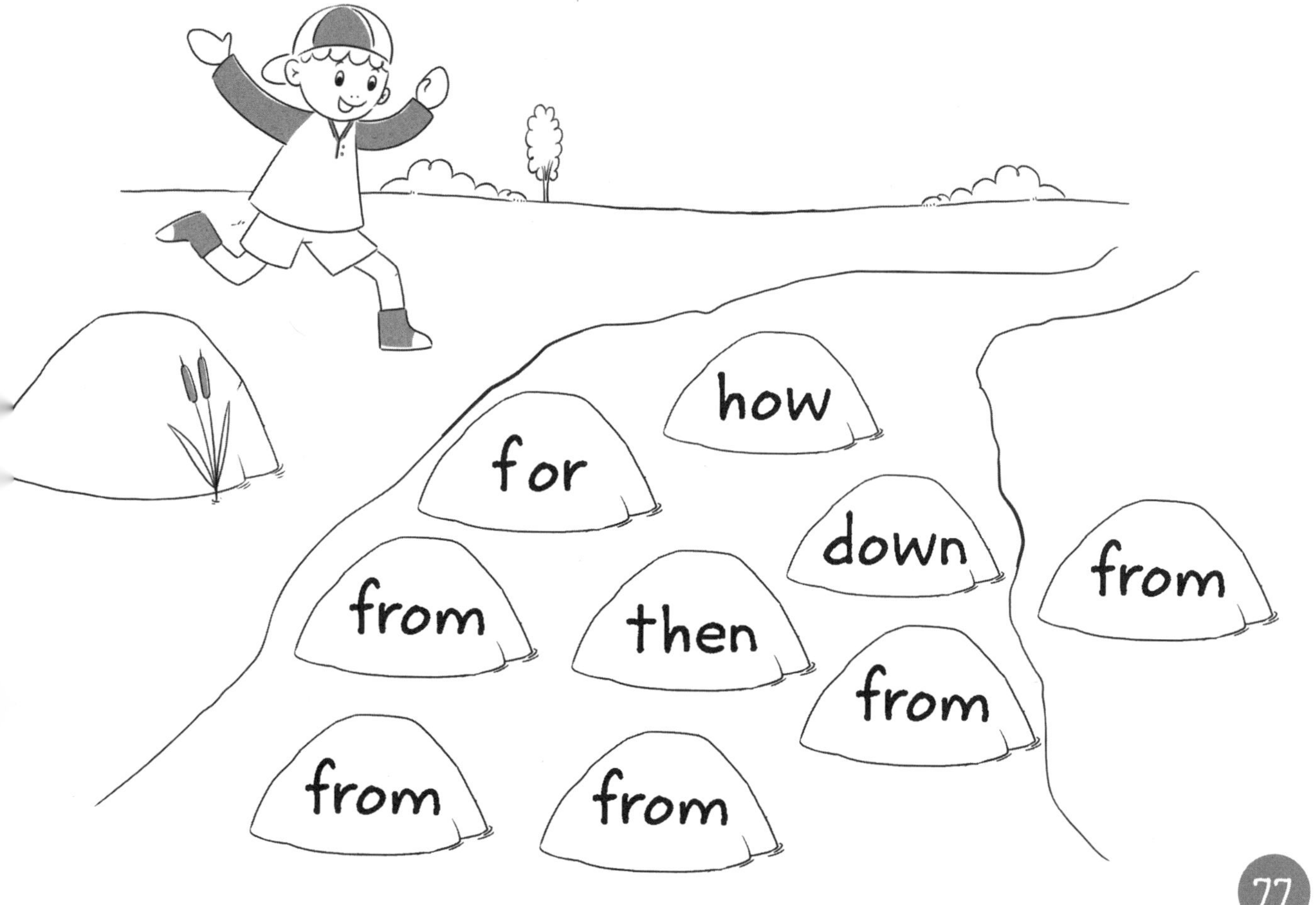

went

Trace the word.

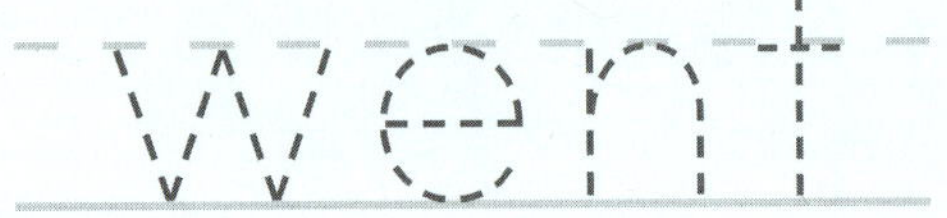

Write it two times.

Read the sentences. Circle the word *went*.

The vet went in the van.

Kim went in a cab.

said

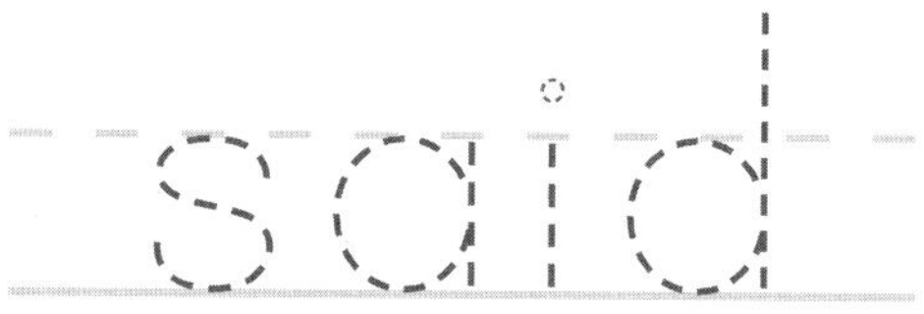

Trace the word.

Write it two times.

Jan's mom **said** it's time to come in. Start at Jan. Draw lines to the word **said** until Jan arrives home.

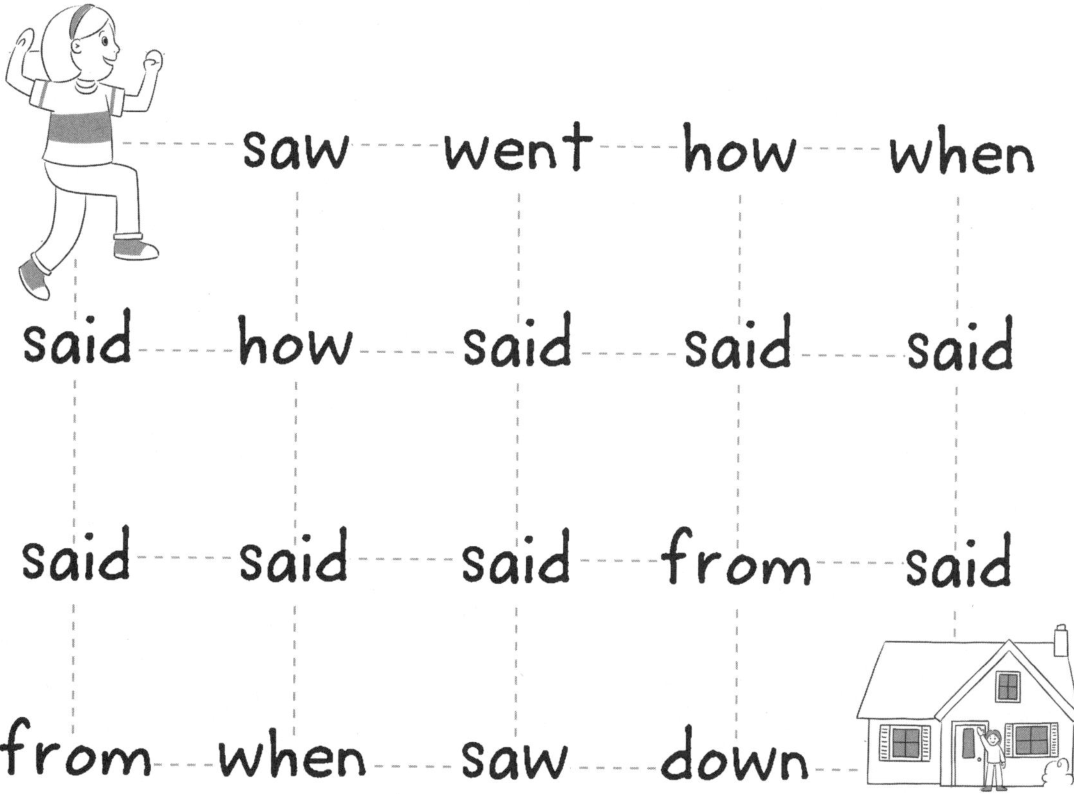

Words in Shapes

Peg is making a big block tower. Each word is on two blocks. Read the words. Color the blocks with matching words the same color.

good

Trace the word.

g o o d

Write it two times.

Which foods taste **good** to you? Draw a line from each food to **good** or **not good** to show what you like.

good

 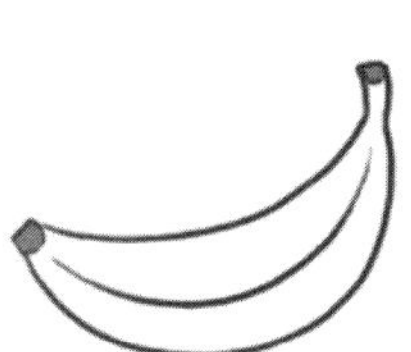  

not good

could

Trace the word.

could

Write it two times.

Fill in the boxes to spell the word **could**. Read the sentences.

The hen ☐☐☐☐☐ fit.

The hen and frog ☐☐☐☐☐ not.

82

little

Trace the word.

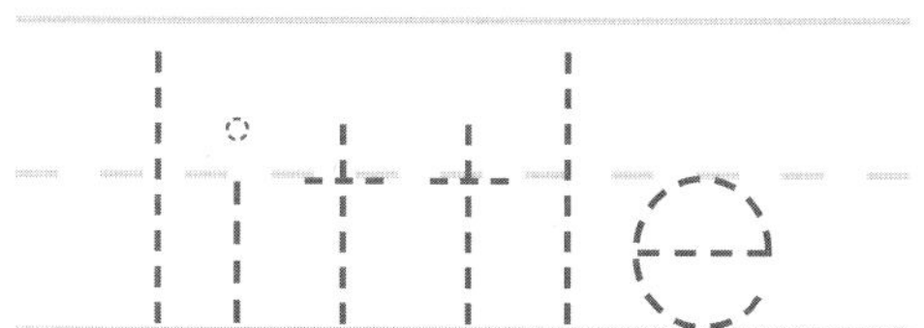

Write it two times.

Color in the word *little*. Then draw a line to the animal that is **little**.

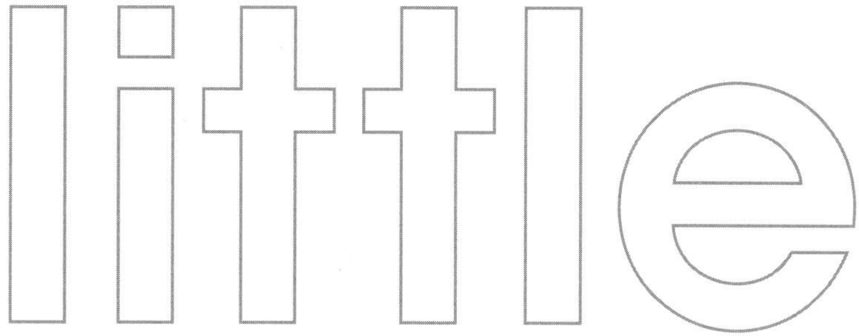

like

Trace the word.

like

Write it two times.

What do you **like**? Decorate *like* with colors and things you **like**!

like

Color by Sight Word

Dot and Sam like to watch the sunrise! Use the color code to color the picture.

good — orange   little — yellow

could — blue   like — green

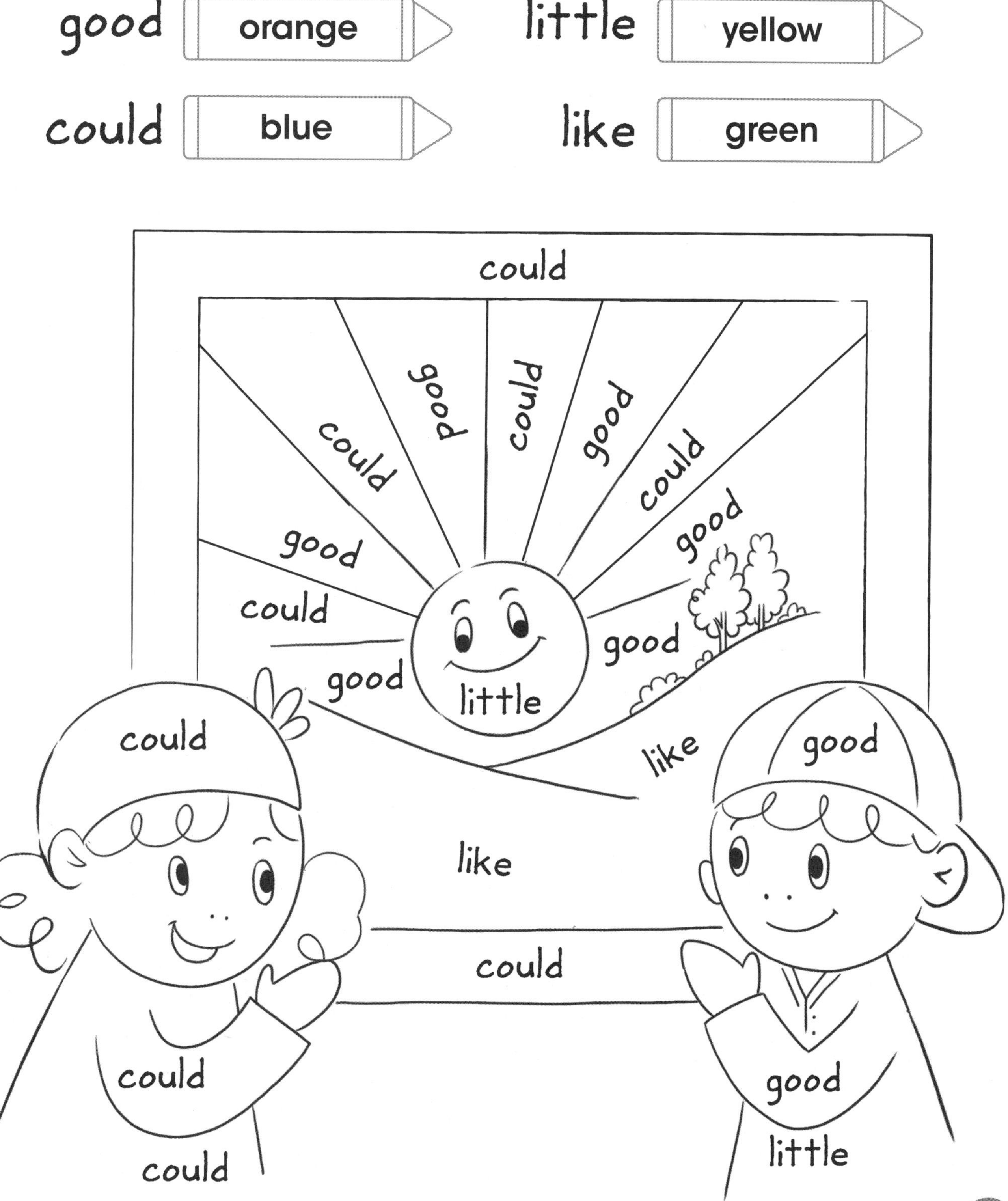

Story Time!

Color the pictures.

Review the sight words.

Read the story.

> down   from   went   said
> good   could   little   like

Tap, Tap!

Tap, tap!
"Who could it be?" said Mat.

Mat went to see. It was Sam!

"Sit down!" said Mat.

Tap, tap!
"What is that from?"
said Sam.

A little bat! "I like bats," said Sam.
"And I like my good pal, Mat."

know

Trace the word.

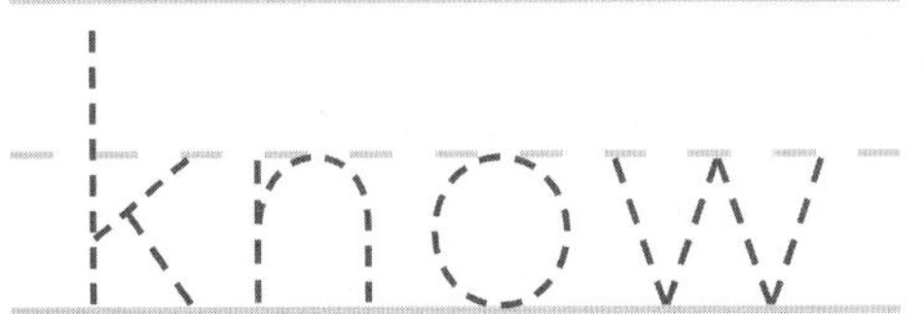

know

Write it two times.

Bud and Jin **know**
the cat is in the box.

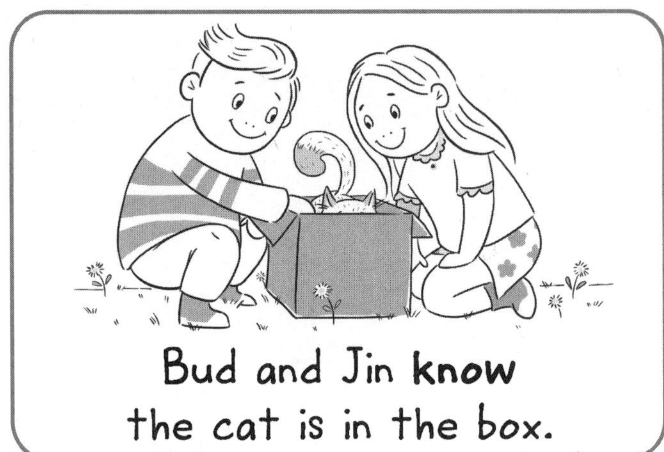

Red **knows** many things because they love to read books! Color in the books with ***know***.

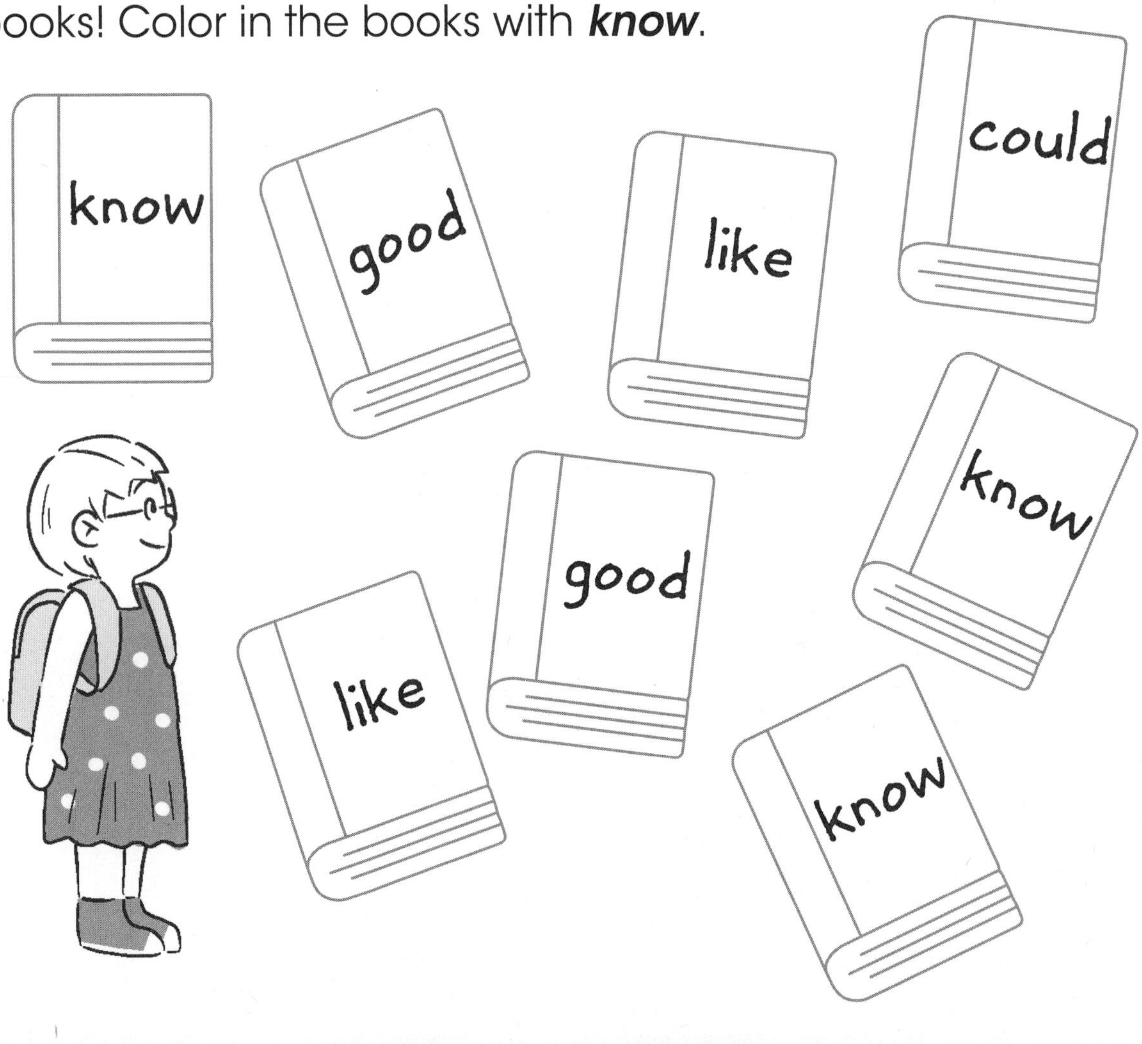

very

Trace the word.

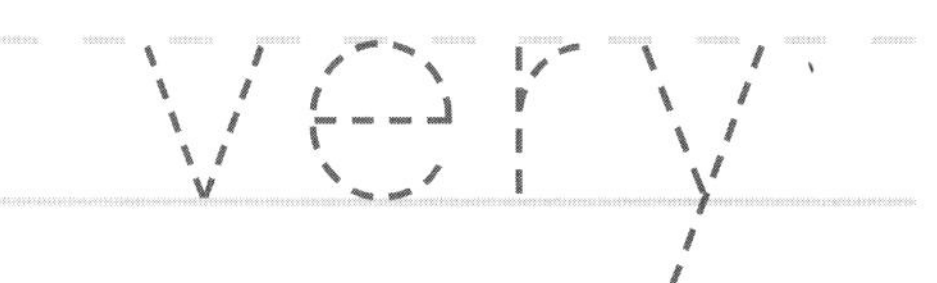

Write it two times.

That pie smells **very** good to Mag! Make a path to the pie. Find **very** hidden three times on the picnic blanket and color in the squares.

x	s	q	v	e	r	y
y	o	v	v	r	y	n
l	d	l	e	i	t	q
t	c	m	r	l	h	e
s	n	c	y	f	x	r
v	e	r	y	e	j	m

some

Trace the word.

Write it two times.

Ben is hungry for **some** dinner! Circle the bowls that have the word **some**.

where

Trace the word.

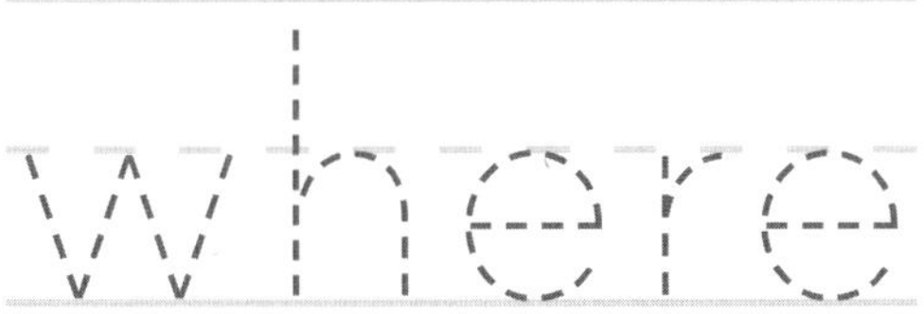

Write it two times.

Fill in the boxes to spell the word **where**.
Read the sentences.

The frog went

it was wet.

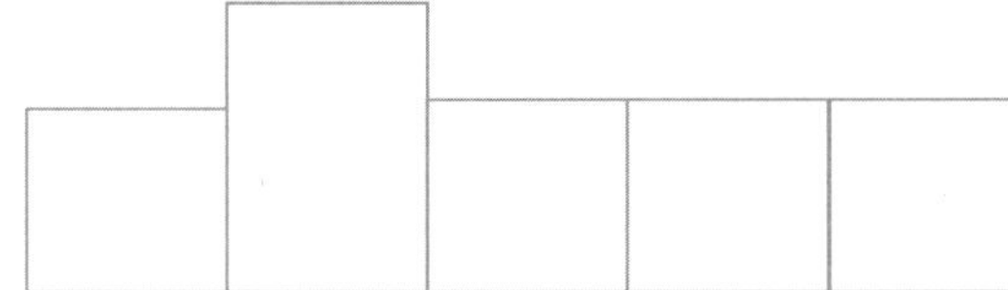

is Mac?

Story Time!

Color the pictures.

Review the sight words.

Read the story.

know	very
some	where

Where Is Jin?

Nic's pals ran and hid.

Some hid in a van.

Some hid in a hut.

"I do not know where
Jin is," said Nic.

Pop! There she is!

"You hid very well, Jin! You win!"

Sight Word List

Aa
all
and
are
as
at

Bb
be
but

Cc
could

Dd
do
down

Ff
for
from

Gg
get
go
good

Hh
had
have
he
his
how

Ii
in

Kk
know

Ll
like
little
look

Mm
my

Nn
now

Oo
of
off
on
or
out

Ss
said
saw
see
she
so
some

Tt
that
the
them
then
there
they
this
to

Uu
up

Vv
very

Ww
was
we
went
were
what
when
where
who
with

Yy
you

"I read the whole book!"®

____

Name

worked hard and finished the

Sight Words